EXPO
2010
SHANGHAI
CHINA

城市，让生活更美好
Better City, Better Life

A bird's - eye view of the site of Expo 2010 Shanghai China

EXPO 2010 SHANGHAI CHINA
OFFICIAL GUIDEBOOK

Bureau of Shanghai World Expo Coordination

China Publishing Group Corporation

EXPO 2010 SHANGHAI CHINA

Full title: The World Exposition Shanghai China 2010

Short title: Expo 2010 Shanghai China

              Expo 2010

              Shanghai Expo

Type: Registered International Exhibition to

              International Exhibitions Bureau

Theme: Better City, Better Life

Duration: May 1 — October 31, 2010

Area: 5.28 km^2

EXPO

2010

SHANGHAI CHINA

The emblem for Expo 2010 Shanghai China resembles the Chinese character "世" (meaning "the world") and has the image of three people holding hands, looking like a happy family. It symbolizes the big family of mankind in harmony and happiness, conveys the world expositions' notion of "understanding, communication, reunion and cooperation", and showcases the great efforts of Expo 2010 Shanghai China to focus on the humanistic core.

The mascot for Expo 2010 Shanghai China, HAIBAO (literally "sea treasure"), is created from the Chinese character "人" (meaning "people"), which reflects the feature of Chinese culture and echoes the Expo's emblem design.

The blue color: implying inclusiveness and imagination, symbolizing China which is full of hope and potential of development.

Hair: resembling the rolling waves, lively and distinct, and explaining the mascot's home and origin.

Face: simplistic cartoonish expression, friendly and confident.

Eyes: big, round eyes, shining with expectation.

Body: round body, evoking beautiful feelings for harmonious life, cute and lovely.

Fist: the thumb is raised to praise and welcome friends from the whole world.

Big feet: standing firmly on the ground and giving strong support to the outspread arms, which implies that China has the capability and determination to hold a wonderful world exposition.

The structure of the Chinese character "人" implies mutual support and signifies that beautiful life needs our joint efforts.

Only by supporting each other and living in harmony between man and nature, people and society and people among themselves, can urban life be better.

Publisher's Notes

From May 1 to October 31, 2010, the World Exposition Shanghai China 2010 will be staged in Shanghai. This is yet another mega event hosted by China following the Beijing Olympics and attracts over 200 countries and international organizations. Through exhibitions, forums and a wide range of events, it provides an opportunity for people to discuss the development of cities, offers their visions for the future, and promotes the communication and cooperation between nations and between cultures.

To better serve visitors and participants from the world, the Bureau of Shanghai World Expo Coordination compiles the Official Guidebook. It provides comprehensive information on exhibitions, events, forums, ticketing, transport, catering, shopping and other services within the Expo Site.

The book includes information submitted before March 25, 2010. Except for theme pavilions and China Pavilion, all the other pavilions are listed in alphabetic order.

Bureau of Shanghai World Expo Coordination

March 2010

Expo 2010 Shanghai China
Confirmed participating countries
and international organizations

Up to March 25, 2010, 242 countries and international organizations have confirmed their participation in Expo 2010.

Countries

China, Afghanistan, Albania, Algeria, Angola, Antigua and Barbuda, Argentina, Armenia, Australia, Austria, Azerbaijan, Bahamas, Bahrain, Bangladesh, Barbados, Belarus, Belgium, Belize, Benin, Bhutan, Bolivia, Bosnia and Herzegovina, Botswana, Brazil, Brunei Darussalam, Bulgaria, Burkina Faso, Burundi, Cambodia, Cameroon, Canada, Cape Verde, Central African Republic, Chad, Chile, Columbia, Comoros, Congo (Republic of the), Cook Islands, Costa Rica, Côte d'Ivoire, Croatia, Cuba, Cyprus, Czech Republic, Democratic People's Republic of Korea, Democratic Republic of the Congo, Denmark, Djibouti, Dominica, Dominican Republic, Ecuador, Egypt, El Salvador, Equatorial Guinea, Eritrea, Estonia, Ethiopia, Fiji, Finland, France, Gabon, Gambia, Georgia, Germany, Ghana, Greece, Grenada, Guatemala, Guinea, Guinea-Bissau, Guyana, Haiti, Honduras, Hungary, Iceland, India, Indonesia, Iran, Iraq, Ireland, Israel, Italy, Jamaica, Japan, Jordan, Kazakhstan, Kenya, Kiribati, Kuwait, Kyrgyzstan, Lao People's Democratic Republic, Latvia, Lebanon, Lesotho, Liberia, Libya, Liechtenstein, Lithuania, Luxembourg, Madagascar, Malawi, Malaysia, Maldives, Mali, Malta, Marshall Islands, Mauritania, Mauritius, Mexico, Micronesia (Federated States of), Monaco, Mongolia, Montenegro, Morocco, Mozambique, Myanmar, Namibia, Nauru, Nepal, Netherlands, New Zealand, Nicaragua, Niger, Nigeria, Niue, Norway, Oman, Pakistan, Palau, Palestine, Panama, Papua New Guinea, Paraguay, Peru, Philippines, Poland, Portugal, Qatar, Republic of Korea, Republic of Moldova, Romania, Russian Federation, Rwanda, Saint Kitts and Nevis, Saint Lucia, Saint Vincent and the Grenadines, Samoa, San Marino, Saudi Arabia, Senegal, Serbia, Seychelles, Sierra Leone, Singapore, Slovakia, Slovenia, Solomon Islands, Somalia, South Africa, Spain, Sri Lanka, Sudan, Suriname, Sweden, Switzerland, Syrian Arab Republic, Tajikistan, Thailand, The Former Yugoslav Republic of Macedonia, Timor-Leste, Togo, Tonga, Trinidad and Tobago, Tunisia, Turkey, Turkmenistan, Tuvalu, Uganda, Ukraine, United Arab Emirates, United Kingdom, United Republic of Tanzania, United States of America, Uruguay, Uzbekistan, Vanuatu, Venezuela, Vietnam, Yemen, Zambia, Zimbabwe

International organizations

African Union Commission, Association of Southeast Asian Nations, Boao Forum for Asia, Caribbean Community, Caribbean Development Bank, Common Market for Eastern and Southern Africa, Commonwealth of Independent States, European Organization for the Exploitation of Meteorological Satellites, European Union, Food and Agriculture Organization of the United Nations, Forum Francophone des Affaires, Global Environment Facility, Group on Earth Observations, International Association of Public Transport, International Atomic Energy Agency, International Council of Museums, International Development Information Network Association, International Energy Agency, International Federation of Red Cross and Red Crescent Societies, International Maritime Organization, International Network for Bamboo and Rattan, International Telecommunication Union, Joint United Nations Program on HIV/AIDS, League of Arab States, Organisation for Economic Cooperation and Development, Pacific Islands Forum, Convention on Biological Diversity, Shanghai Cooperation Organization, South Pacific Tourism Organization, UN Framework Convention on Climate Change, UN Habitat, United Cities and Local Governments, United Nations, United Nations Capital Development Fund, United Nations Children's Fund, United Nations Conference on Trade and Development, United Nations Educational, Scientific and Cultural Organization, United Nations Environment Program, United Nations High Commissioner for Refugees, United Nations Industrial Development Organization, United Nations Population Fund, World Bank, World Health Organization, World Intellectual Property Organization, World Meteorological Organization, World Tourism Organization, World Trade Centers Association, World Trade Organization, World Water Council, World Wide Fund for Nature

Expo 2010 Shanghai China

Themed "Better City, Better Life", Expo 2010 is the first world exposition that focuses on the issues of city. Governments and people from all over the world will meet in Shanghai to discuss cities' cultural achievements, development practices and advanced concepts, explore brand-new housing, living and working models in the new century and showcase interesting examples of sustainable development and harmonious society.

Exhibitions ⇢ P14
Amazing exhibitions in the pavilions will provide visitors with an unforgettable experience.

Events ⇢ P170
Various kinds of cultural activities and artistic performances across the world are gathered in the Expo site to make Expo 2010 a feast of the cultural exchange of the world.

Forums ⇢ P182
Forums as an important part of Expo spiritual heritage provide a vision for the future.

Landmarks ⇢ P186
Eye-catching buildings and lovely greenery creat a kind of bright scenery in Expo site.

Services ⇢ P198
The Organizer commits to providing the most considerate services to maximize visitors' satisfaction.

Expo Shanghai Online ⇢ P218
Log on to the Expo Shanghai Online, and start a fantastic virtual tour.

Expo 2010 is staged in an area between Nanpu Bridge and Lupu Bridge along both sides of the Huangpu River in downtown Shanghai. It has five zones, with zones A, B and C in Pudong, and D and E in Puxi.

Zone A	Pavilions of some Asian nations, etc.
Zone B	Urbanian Pavilion, Pavilion of City Being, Pavilion of Urban Planet, pavilions of some Asian nations, pavilions of Oceanian nations, pavilions of international organizations, etc.
Zone C	Pavilions of European, American and African nations, etc.
Zone D	Pavilion of Footprint, pavilions of enterprises, etc.
Zone E	Pavilion of Future, pavilions of enterprises, UBPA, etc.

Exhibitions

⋯⋙Theme Pavilions

Urbanian Pavilion	. . . 17	Pavilion of Footprint	. . . 20
Pavilion of City Being	. . . 18	Pavilion of Future	. . . 21
Pavilion of Urban Planet	. . . 19		

⋯⋙Pavilions in Zone A

China Pavilion	. . . 24	Beijing Pavilion	. . . 35
Asia Joint Pavilion I	. . . 26	Tianjin Pavilion	. . . 35
Bangladesh Pavilion	. . . 26	Hebei Pavilion	. . . 35
Kyrgyzstan Pavilion	. . . 27	Shanxi Pavilion	. . . 36
Maldives Pavilion	. . . 27	Inner Mongolia Pavilion	. . . 36
Mongolia Pavilion	. . . 28	Liaoning Pavilion	. . . 36
Tajikistan Pavilion	. . . 28	Jilin Pavilion	. . . 37
Timor-Leste Pavilion	. . . 29	Heilongjiang Pavilion	. . . 37
Asia Joint Pavilion II	. . . 29	Jiangsu Pavilion	. . . 37
Afghanistan Pavilion	. . . 30	Zhejiang Pavilion	. . . 38
Bahrain Pavilion	. . . 30	Anhui Pavilion	. . . 38
Jordan Pavilion	. . . 31	Fujian Pavilion	. . . 38
Palestine Pavilion	. . . 31	Jiangxi Pavilion	. . . 39
Syria Pavilion	. . . 32	Shandong Pavilion	. . . 39
Yemen Pavilion	. . . 32	Henan Pavilion	. . . 39
Asia Joint Pavilion III	. . . 33	Hubei Pavilion	. . . 40
Laos Pavilion	. . . 33	Hunan Pavilion	. . . 40
Myanmar Pavilion	. . . 34	Guangdong Pavilion	. . . 40
Chinese Provinces Joint Pavilion	. . . 34	Guangxi Pavilion	. . . 41

Contents

Hainan Pavilion . . . 41

Chongqing Pavilion . . . 41

Sichuan Pavilion . . . 42

Guizhou Pavilion . . . 42

Yunnan Pavilion . . . 42

Tibet Pavilion . . . 43

Shaanxi Pavilion . . . 43

Gansu Pavilion . . . 43

Qinghai Pavilion . . . 44

Ningxia Pavilion . . . 44

Xinjiang Pavilion . . . 44

Shanghai Pavilion . . . 45

Democratic People's Republic
of Korea Pavilion . . . 45

Hong Kong Pavilion . . . 46

India Pavilion . . . 46

Iran Pavilion . . . 47

Israel Pavilion . . . 47

Japan Pavilion . . . 48

Kazakhstan Pavilion . . . 48

Lebanon Pavilion . . . 49

Macao Pavilion . . . 49

Morocco Pavilion . . . 50

Nepal Pavilion . . . 50

Oman Pavilion . . . 51

Pakistan Pavilion . . . 51

Qatar Pavilion . . . 52

Republic of Korea Pavilion . . . 52

Saudi Arabia Pavilion . . . 53

Sri Lanka Pavilion . . . 53

Taiwan Pavilion . . . 54

Turkmenistan Pavilion . . . 54

UAE Pavilion . . . 55

Uzbekistan Pavilion . . . 55

Vietnam Pavilion . . . 56

Pavilions in Zone B

Australia Pavilion . . . 60

Brunei Darussalam Pavilion . . . 60

Cambodia Pavilion . . . 61

DEVNET Pavilion . . . 61

International Red Cross and Red Crescent
Pavilion . . . 62

Indonesia Pavilion . . . 62

Joint Pavilion of International
Organizations . . . 63

Pavilion of Association of Southeast
Asian Nations . . . 63

Pavilion of Boao Forum for Asia . . . 64

Pavilion of Common Market for
Eastern and Southern Africa   . . . 64
Pavilion of Forum Francophone
des Affaires   . . . 65
Pavilion of Global Environment Facility. . . 65
Pavilion of International Association
of Public Transport   . . . 66
Pavilion of International Council
of Museums   . . . 66
Pavilion of International Network
for Bamboo and Rattan   . . . 67
Pavilion of League of Arab States   . . . 67
Pavilion of Shanghai Cooperation
Organization   . . . 68
Pavilion of United Cities and Local
Governments   . . . 68

Pavilion of World Water Council   . . . 69
Pavilion of World Wide Fund
for Nature   . . . 69
Life Sunshine Pavilion   . . . 70
Malaysia Pavilion   . . . 70
MeteoWorld Pavilion   . . . 71
New Zealand Pavilion   . . . 71
Pacific Joint Pavilion   . . . 72
Pavilion of Public Participation   . . . 72
Pavilion of World Trade Centers
Association   . . . 73
Philippines Pavilion   . . . 73
Singapore Pavilion   . . . 74
Thailand Pavilion   . . . 74
UN Joint Pavilion   . . . 75

⋯⋗Pavilions in Zone C

Africa Pavilion   . . . 78
African Union (AU) Pavilion   . . . 78
Benin Pavilion   . . . 79
Botswana Pavilion   . . . 79
Burundi Pavilion   . . . 80
Cameroon Pavilion   . . . 80
Cape Verde Pavilion   . . . 81

Central African Republic Pavilion   . . . 81
Chad Pavilion   . . . 82
Comoros Pavilion   . . . 82
Republic of the Congo Pavilion   . . . 83
Côte d'Ivoire Pavilion   . . . 83
Democratic Republic of the
Congo Pavilion   . . . 84

Djibouti Pavilion	. . . 84	Sudan Pavilion	. . . 97
Equatorial Guinea Pavilion	. . . 85	Togo Pavilion	. . . 97
Eritrea Pavilion	. . . 85	Uganda Pavilion	. . . 98
Ethiopia Pavilion	. . . 86	Tanzania Pavilion	. . . 98
Gabon Pavilion	. . . 86	Zambia Pavilion	. . . 99
Gambia Pavilion	. . . 87	Zimbabwe Pavilion	. . . 99
Ghana Pavilion	. . . 87	Algeria Pavilion	. . . 100
Guinea Pavilion	. . . 88	Angola Pavilion	. . . 100
Guinea-Bissau Pavilion	. . . 88	Argentina Pavilion	. . . 101
Kenya Pavilion	. . . 89	Austria Pavilion	. . . 101
Lesotho Pavilion	. . . 89	Belarus Pavilion	. . . 102
Liberia Pavilion	. . . 90	Belgium-EU Pavilion	. . . 102
Madagascar Pavilion	. . . 90	Bosnia and Herzegovina Pavilion	. . . 103
Malawi Pavilion	. . . 91	Brazil Pavilion	. . . 103
Mali Pavilion	. . . 91	Canada Pavilion	. . . 104
Mauritania Pavilion	. . . 92	Caribbean Community Joint Pavilion	. . . 104
Mauritius Pavilion	. . . 92	Antigua and Barbuda Pavilion	. . . 105
Mozambique Pavilion	. . . 93	Bahamas Pavilion	. . . 105
Namibia Pavilion	. . . 93	Barbados Pavilion	. . . 106
Niger Pavilion	. . . 94	Belize Pavilion	. . . 106
Rwanda Pavilion	. . . 94	Caribbean Community Pavilion	. . . 107
Senegal Pavilion	. . . 95	Caribbean Development Bank	
Seychelles Pavilion	. . . 95	Pavilion	. . . 107
Sierra Leone Pavilion	. . . 96	Dominica Pavilion	. . . 108
Somalia Pavilion	. . . 96	Grenada Pavilion	. . . 108

Guyana Pavilion . . . 109

Haiti Pavilion . . . 109

Jamaica Pavilion . . . 110

Saint Kitts and Nevis Pavilion . . . 110

Saint Lucia Pavilion . . . 111

Saint Vincent and the Grenadines

   Pavilion . . . 111

Suriname Pavilion . . . 112

Trinidad and Tobago Pavilion . . . 112

Chile Pavilion . . . 113

Colombia Pavilion . . . 113

Croatia Pavilion . . . 114

Cuba Pavilion . . . 114

Czech Pavilion . . . 115

Denmark Pavilion . . . 115

Egypt Pavilion . . . 116

Estonia Pavilion . . . 116

Europe Joint Pavilion I . . . 117

   Cyprus Pavilion . . . 117

   Liechtenstein Pavilion . . . 118

   Malta Pavilion . . . 118

   San Marino Pavilion . . . 119

Europe Joint Pavilion II . . . 119

   Albania Pavilion . . . 120

   Armenia Pavilion . . . 120

Azerbaijan Pavilion . . . 121

Bulgaria Pavilion . . . 121

Georgia Pavilion . . . 122

Montenegro Pavilion . . . 122

Moldova Pavilion . . . 123

Former Yugoslav Republic of

   Macedonia Pavilion . . . 123

Finland Pavilion . . . 124

France Pavilion . . . 124

Germany Pavilion . . . 125

Greece Pavilion . . . 125

Hungary Pavilion . . . 126

Iceland Pavilion . . . 126

Ireland Pavilion . . . 127

Italy Pavilion . . . 127

Joint Pavilion of Central and South

   American Countries . . . 128

   Bolivia Pavilion . . . 128

   Costa Rica Pavilion . . . 129

   Dominican Republic Pavilion . . . 129

   Ecuador Pavilion . . . 130

   El Salvador Pavilion . . . 130

   Guatemala Pavilion . . . 131

   Honduras Pavilion . . . 131

   Nicaragua Pavilion . . . 132

Panama Pavilion	. . . 132	Russia Pavilion	. . . 140
Uruguay Pavilion	. . . 133	Serbia Pavilion	. . . 140
Latvia Pavilion	. . . 133	Slovakia Pavilion	. . . 141
Libya Pavilion	. . . 134	Slovenia Pavilion	. . . 141
Lithuania Pavilion	. . . 134	South Africa Pavilion	. . . 142
Luxembourg Pavilion	. . . 135	Spain Pavilion	. . . 142
Mexico Pavilion	. . . 135	Sweden Pavilion	. . . 143
Monaco Pavilion	. . . 136	Swiss Pavilion	. . . 143
The Netherlands Pavilion	. . . 136	Tunisia Pavilion	. . . 144
Nigeria Pavilion	. . . 137	Turkey Pavilion	. . . 144
Norway Pavilion	. . . 137	Ukraine Pavilion	. . . 145
Peru Pavilion	. . . 138	UK Pavilion	. . . 145
Poland Pavilion	. . . 138	US Pavilion	. . . 146
Portugal Pavilion	. . . 139	Venezuela Pavilion	. . . 146
Romania Pavilion	. . . 139		

Pavilions in Zone D

Aurora Pavilion	. . . 150	PICC Pavilion	. . . 153
China Railway Pavilion	. . . 150	Republic of Korea Business Pavilion	. . . 153
China Oil Pavilion	. . . 151	Shanghai Corporate Pavilion	. . . 154
Cisco Pavilion	. . . 151	Space Home Pavilion	. . . 154
Coca Cola Pavilion	. . . 152	State Grid Pavilion	. . . 155
Japanese Industry Pavilion	. . . 152		

Pavilions in Zone E

Broad Pavilion . . . 158

China Aviation Pavilion . . . 158

CSSC Pavilion . . . 159

Information and Communication
Pavilion . . . 159

Private Enterprises Pavilion . . . 160

SAIC-GM Pavilion . . . 160

Vanke Pavilion . . . 161

Urban Best Practices Area (UBPA) . . . 162

   Built Cases (Northern Part) . . . 163

   Alsace Case Pavilion . . . 163

   Chengdu Case Pavilion . . . 163

   Hamburg Case Pavilion . . . 163

London Case Pavilion . . . 164

Macao Case Pavilion . . . 164

Madrid Case Pavilion . . . 164

Makkah Case Pavilion . . . 165

Ningbo Case Pavilion . . . 165

Odense Case Pavilion . . . 165

Rhône-Alpes Case Pavilion . . . 166

Rhône-Alpes Lighting Case Pavilion . . . 166

Shanghai Case Pavilion . . . 166

Vancouver Case Pavilion . . . 167

Xi'an Case Pavilion . . . 167

Cases in Pavilion (Central Part) . . . 167

Other Cases (Southern Part) . . . 169

Events

Events Provided by the Organizer . . . 172

Events by Participants . . . 178

Forums

Summit Forum . . . 182

Theme Forums . . . 183

   Theme forum I: Information Technology
and Urban Development . . . 183

Theme forum II: Cultural Heritage and
Urban Regeneration . . . 183

Theme forum III: Science & Technology
Innovation and Urban Future . . . 184

Theme forum IV: Urban Responsibilities
during Environmental Changes . . . 184
Theme forum V: Economic Transformation
and Urban-rural Relations . . . 184

Theme forum VI: Harmonious City and
Liveable Life . . . 185
Public Forum . . . 185

Landmarks

Expo Center . . . 188
Expo Axis . . . 189
Expo Culture Center . . . 190
World Exposition Museum . . . 191
Bao Steel Stage . . . 192

Entertainment Hall . . . 193
Bailianjing Garden . . . 194
Houtan Garden . . . 195
Expo Garden . . . 196

Services

Ticketing . . . 200
Transportation . . . 203
Catering . . . 208

Shopping . . . 213
Visitor services . . . 214
Volunteers . . . 216

Expo Shanghai Online

Expo Shanghai Online . . . 220

Exhibitions

Events

Forums

Landmarks

Services

Expo Shanghai Online

The fantastic exhibitions in the theme pavilions, national pavilions, international organizations' pavilions, pavilions of enterprises and UBPA will be the core elements of an Expo Site tour. They will work together to deliver the message of "Better City, Better Life".

Theme Pavilions

Expo 2010 will have five theme pavilions, namely, Urbanian, City Being, Urban Planet, Footprint and Future. The first three are housed in the Theme Pavilion building in Zone B where is one of the Expo landmarks, for which the designing is inspired by the concept of the "paper folding". As an attractive feature, the roof is designed to imitate the dormer window that is often found in Shikumen houses (a traditional Shanghai architectural style). During the period of Expo, a wide range of events and ceremonies will be held in the building's three squares. The other two pavilions, Footprint and Future, are located in two modified industrial buildings in Zone D and Zone E respectively; they represent a fascinating mix of tradition and modernity.

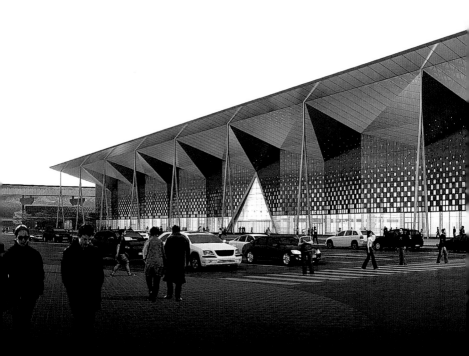

Urbanian Pavilion

Theme: Overall human development is a prerequisite for sustainable development of cities

Urbanian Pavilion, focusing on the needs and development of people, tells the stories of people in cities. In its five sections, i.e. "Family", "Work", "Contact", "Learning" and "Health", visitors will see the videos of six real families from six cities of five continents. Together with the exhibits, settings and multimedia installations, the sight of 11 cities are racily showed. Visitors will have a vivid view of city dwellers' life and it is the pursuiting of a better life that draws people to urban areas.

- In the Family section, the mirrors mounted from floor to ceiling create 3-dimension pictures, as if providing visitors a window through which they can observe the lives of the six families.

- A gigantic machine, metaphorized as "factory, stock exchange and clock" is installed in the Work section. Screens of varying sizes are mounted on it to demonstrate how people work in different cities.
- The Contact section uses a full-dome screen to create a projection of 360° to show the social life of different family members.
- The Learning section creates a circumstance resembling the traditional classroom and library, and shows the learning experiences of family members and the educational and cultural facilities in cities.
- The Health section shows the videos and other data concerning the health of family members and creates an environment that is clean, fresh and healthy.

Pavilion of City Being

Theme: **The city, like a living being, needs the protection of humanity to remain healthy**

The pavilion is situated in the Theme Pavilion building in Zone B. The theme of life, or the city's journey of life, runs through all its exhibitions. In a metaphorical way with high scientific technologies, a city is compared to a living being consisting of body and soul. Metabolism and circulation are important for it to function properly. Constant adjustment between man and a city is the key for the health of the city being.

- "Vigor Station" has five "kiosks" which represent population, logistics, energy, finance and information. The LCD display shows, on a real-time basis, the train, flight, ship, stock and foreign exchange information in the world's major cities.
- "Circulation System" leads visitors through vast underground pipes. The Pipeline section has many interactive features to highlight the vulnerability of cities and inspire visitors to contemplate their responsibilities towards the protection of cities.
- The City Plazas section features movies about five world-renowned city plazas and provides a clue to the cultural identities of different cities.
- The "library" in the City Street section tries to use ten books to show how ten cities' rise or fall impacts the life of people.

Pavilion of Urban Planet

Theme: Humanity in symbiosis with city and planet

The pavilion is located in the Theme Pavilion building in Zone B. The top of two parallel spiral ramps offers a good view of a 32m-diameter globe. Its five sections including "Blue Planet" and "The Only Planet We Have" tell how the development, sometimes overdevelopment, of cities produces ecological problems, and how people awaken to urbanization and environmental challenges. Visitors come to understand cities as a source of both problems and solutions.

- Blue Planet is a huge globe that represents the earth. In a poetic and metaphorical way, it tells how cities, urban development and human behaviors impact the earth.
- "The Only Planet We Have" is an interesting short movie about the interaction between cities, the earth and people.

Pavilion of Footprint

Theme: **Footprints left as a result of people's interaction with cities and the environment from the birth of the world's cities to modern civilization**

The Pavilion is located in Zone D and includes three exhibition halls: "City's Origin", "Growing City" and "Urban Wisdom". It traces the birth and growth of cities, their philosophies and the urban wisdom centering innovation and harmony.

- City's Origin Hall shows what cities looked like in the early agrarian era. Visitors may have a chance to understand the reasons behind the formation of cities including those along Yangtze and Yellow Rivers, ancient worship systems, patron saints of ancient cities, etc.
- Growing City Hall shows full-blown cities, including Florence, Amsterdam, Byzantium and Istanbul. Visitors may have a chance to see ancient streets in China's Song Dynasty and Japan's Edo Period, and know more about urban development achievements in Tibet and about the Forbidden City in Beijing.
- Urban Wisdom Hall deals with the Industrial Revolution era. Industrialization is depicted as a double-edged sword that changes the life in cities. New York and London are cited as two examples of innovative wisdom. The exhibition also includes the culture of the Chinese Grand Canal and the urban renewal efforts in Shanghai.

Pavilion of Future

Theme: Dream inspires the future of cities

The Pavilion is located in Zone E. The exhibition starts with an interaction with visitors, inviting them to imagine what cities will be like in the future. Through movies, books and sculptures, it tells how a city was envisaged, planned and realized in history, proposes the various possibilities of a future city, and points to the spiritual elements that have always driven human progress.

- Dream of Yesterday section features a gigantic screen for science-fiction movies.
- Dream and Practice section uses digital books to present how people used to depict future cities. Nine sculptures are displayed to echo the theme of better city.
- In the Multiple Possibilities section, an animated film is shown at a 36-meter-high screen. Five dreamlike street settings, namely Ecological City, City of Wisdom, City of Water, Space City and City of Energy, displayed on the background around, describe the various possibilities of city development and life in the future.
- The displays in the Dream Is Approaching section focus on Intelligent Home, Healthy Community, Low-Carbon City and Harmonious Environment. They will help visitors to understand the trend of technological advancement.

Location Diagram of Pavilions in Zone A

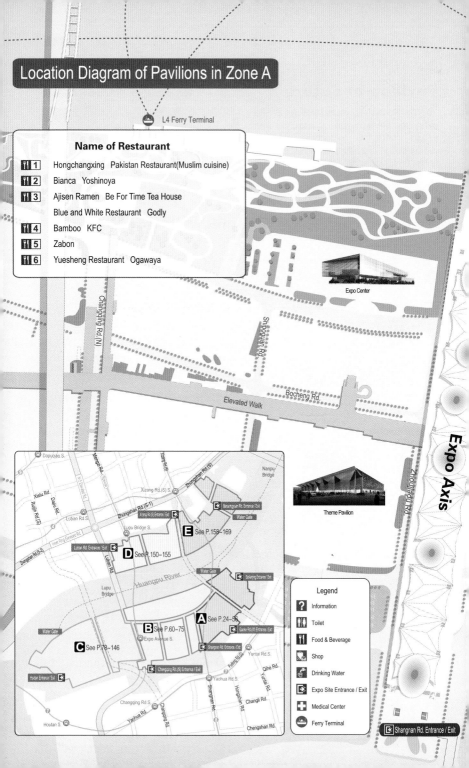

L4 Ferry Terminal

Name of Restaurant

🍴1	Hongchangxing Pakistan Restaurant(Muslim cuisine)
🍴2	Bianca Yoshinoya
🍴3	Ajisen Ramen Be For Time Tea House
	Blue and White Restaurant Godly
🍴4	Bamboo KFC
🍴5	Zabon
🍴6	Yuesheng Restaurant Ogawaya

Expo Center

Changgong Rd.(N)

Shangshan Rd.

Bocheng Rd.

Elevated Walk

Nanpu Bridge

Theme Pavilion

Expo Axis

Zhoujiadu Rd.

(Inset map)

Dapuqiao S.

Xielu Rd.

Ruijin Rd.(S)

Dapu Rd.

Menghu Rd.(S)(Shi)

Yaong Rd.(S)

Xuzang Rd.(S) S

Zhongshan Rd.(S)

Luban Rd.S.

Zhongshan Rd.(S-1)

Jirong Rd.(S) Entrance / Exit

Lupu Bridge S.

Balaxinguan Rd. Entrance / Exit

Water Gate

E See P.158~169

Lution Rd. Entrance / Exit

D See P.150~155

Zhongshan Rd.(S-2)

Luban Rd.

Lupu Bridge

Huangpu River

Water Gate

Bailiang Entrance / Exit

Water Gate

B See P.60~75

C See P.78~146

Expo Avenue S.

A See P.24~59

Gaoke Rd.(W) Entrance / Exit

Houtan Entrance / Exit

Changgong Rd.(N) Entrance / Exit

Shangnan Rd. Entrance / Exit

Changqing Rd.S.

Changqing Rd.

Yaohua Rd.

Yaohua Rd. S.

Hongshan Rd.

Puming Rd.(S)

Yuntai Rd.S.

Yudai Rd.

Qihe Rd.

Changli Rd.

Houtan S.

Chengshan Rd.

Legend

❓	Information
🚻	Toilet
🍴	Food & Beverage
🛍	Shop
🚰	Drinking Water
➡	Expo Site Entrance / Exit
➕	Medical Center
⚓	Ferry Terminal

➡ Shangnan Rd. Entrance / Exit

Huangpu River

Water Gate

L2 Ferry Terminal

Waiting Square

Expo Culture Center

Vietnam Pavilion

Japan Pavilion

Asia Joint Pavilion III

Republic of Korea Pavilion

Gaoke Rd.(W)

Xizang Rd.(S) Tunnel

Expo Avenue

1

4

Saudi Arabia Pavilion

India Pavilion

Bailianjing Rd.

Bailianjing Entrance / Exit

Kazakhstan Pavilion

Uzbekistan Pavilion

Asia Joint Pavilion I

2

5

6

Nepal Pavilion

Asia Joint Pavilion II

Theme Square

Elevated Walk

Elevated Walk

Iran Pavilion

Lebanon Pavilion

Democratic People's Republic of Korea Pavilion

Bailian River

Shangnan Rd.

Taiwan Pavilion

3

Sri Lanka Pavilion

Yuntai Rd.

Morocco Pavilion

Turkmenistan Pavilion

Qatar Pavilion

Waiting Square

Israel Pavilion

Pakistan Pavilion

UAE Pavilion

Gaoke Rd.(W) Entrance / Exit

Oman Pavilion

China Pavilion
Chinese Provinces Joint Pavilion

Macao Pavilion

Hong Kong Pavilion

Waiting Square

Guozhan Rd.

Xueye Rd.

Hongshan Rd.

Pudong Rd.(S)

Zone

China Pavilion

Theme: **Chinese Wisdom in Urban Development**

National Day: October 1

Themed on Oriental Crown, Splendid China, Ample Barn, Rich People, the pavilion tries to reveal an ideal that is deep-rooted in Chinese culture.

Consisting of The Footprint, The Dialogue and The Actions sections, China Pavilion's exhibitions will take visitors on a journey of quest, encouraging them to discover and comprehend the Chinese wisdom in evolution of cities. Starting with the country's unprecedented urbanization achievements over the past three decades, the exhibitions seek to shed light on the classical wisdom embodied in China's urban development process. Then visitors are invited to ponder over the future, over an urban development path illuminated by the Chinese values and development outlook.

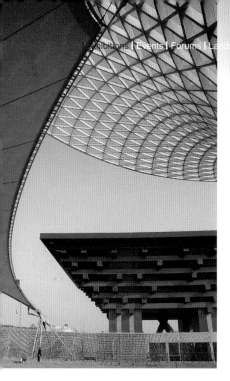

- Section 2: This section features a ride themed as a "dialogue between past and present". It offers a dynamic and exciting tour of discovery, enabling the visitors to find out themselves about the Chinese wisdom in city planning.
- Section 3: The exhibition focuses on a low-carbon lifestyle that will shape the development of Chinese cities in the future. It shows how Chinese are inspired by nature and propose their own solutions to global challenges in urbanization and sustainable development.

- Section 1: In The Footprint section, a short movie tells the experience of Chinese in urbanization over the past three decades, their passion for construction and faith in a bright future; then, a celebrated painting "Along the River during the Qingming Festival" is displayed to reflect the ancient Chinese wisdom about cities.

Asia Joint Pavilion I

Zone

The joint pavilion has the exhibitions of Bangladesh, Kyrgyzstan, Maldives, Mongolia, Tajikistan and Timor-Leste.

Bangladesh Pavilion

Theme: **Spirit and Growth of Golden Bengal**

National Day: September 20

The pavilion entrance is decorated with colorful traditional Bangladeshi patterns. A small sculpture, pictures of new urban areas, and models of traditional architecture symbolize the dialogue between tradition and future.

• Pictures on a wall show the Bangladeshi national features.
• The catering area inside the pavilion provides Bangladeshi food.

Kyrgyzstan Pavilion

Theme: **Bishkek——the City Open to the World**

A

Zone

National Day: August 4

The pavilion, resembling a yurt, symbolizes the harmonious coexistence between the nomadic people and nature. Bishkek, though highly industrial, is a liveable city with large green area. Movies, posters, slides, exhibits and cultural activities in the pavilion introduces the country's culture, history and customs, and the harmonious development of economy, culture and tourism in Bishkek.

- The three sections in the pavilion present the unique characteristics of the country and Bishkek from different perspectives.
- The exhibits demonstrate the capital's achievements in socioeconomic transition and other characteristics of urban construction in the country.
- Local songs and dances are presented during the National Day.

Maldives Pavilion

Theme: **Maldives, Tomorrow**

National Day: June 7

In the past decade, Maldives has grown into a model of tourism and environmental protection with tourism and fishery as the pillars of its urban development. The pavilion showcases the country's modern life by describing the country's efforts in cultural inheritance and environmental protection while developing various industries.

- The distinctive setting and a variety of exhibits unfold the folk culture of the island country.
- The exhibited seafood such as tuna, skipjack, lobster, shark and hawksbill demonstrate the country's rich fishery resources.

Zone

Mongolia Pavilion

Theme: **Gobi and the City**

National Day: September 13

A huge dinosaur egg, symbolizing the fragile city, is laid in the center of the pavilion, implying that the urban development shall be based on ecological balance. Two dinosaur skeleton models and distinctive wooden tents are set up in the egg.

- Models of baby dinosaurs and pictures show information on dinosaur eggs.
- Visitors may experience life inside the tent which is made of wood without a single nail.

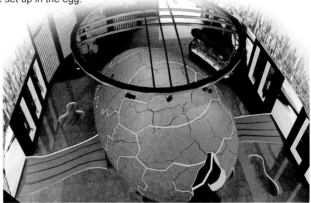

Tajikistan Pavilion

Theme: **The Evolution of City Structure and the Good Life**

National Day: September 22

Tajikistan enjoys 60% of hydropower resource in Central Asia, which is reflected in the pavilion through simulated snow mountains and waterfalls in the natural environment. Models of historical events and architectures are used to depict work and life of people in the mountainous country.

- Abundant images present typical artworks, recent urban construction achievements of Tajikistan and its friendship with neighboring countries.
- The pavilion has a rest area sheltered by grapevines.

Timor-Leste Pavilion

Theme: Be with Us, Be with Nature

A

Zone

National Day: July 13

Lospalos-style roof, carved wooden door, processed palm leaves and a dazzling array of handicrafts depict a unique look of Timor-Leste. With the help of lighting, the country's natural scenery, scenes of work and entertainment of its people are displayed, showing the harmonious coexistence between humanity and nature.

- Modern technologies are applied to recreate a day from dawn to dusk in the country and show people's tranquil and leisure life.
- Various handicrafts such as wood and stone carvings are exhibited.
- Visitors feast their eyes on the performances of local songs and dances.

Asia Joint Pavilion II

The joint pavilion has the exhibitions of Afghanistan, Bahrain, Jordan, Palestine, Syria and Yemen.

Zone A

Afghanistan Pavilion

Theme: **Afghanistan— Heart of Asia, Land of Opportunities & Resources**

National Day: August 19

The Pavilion is a reconstruction of the famous Blue Mosque of Herat. The rich blue and green mosaic tiles take visitors right into the stories of the Oriental Nights and attract them to move inside.

- The Rahimy Collection of Afghan Treasures displays more than 400 unique exhibits. The nomad tent, objects of daily use, antique rugs and textiles, traditional silver jewellery and corals show the time-honoured history and brilliant culture of Afghanistan.
- The bazaar inside the pavilion sells handicrafts, nuts and dry fruits, jewellery, textiles, spices and herbs, etc.

Bahrain Pavilion

Theme: **Small is Beautiful**

National Day: October 22

The pavilion is a classical architecture with a white exterior wall and the curve structure of the internal designing, presenting a charming nation from a special perspective. A curved path accompanied by warm tone and interesting exhibits leads visitors to a tour of discovery from historical culture to modern development and then to the future.

- Ancient craftsmanship is shown in replicas of cultural relics with high archeological value. Also on display are modern and traditional Bahrain jewelries.

- Videos and touch-screen interactions make visitors close to Bahrain's unique way of living and national heritages.

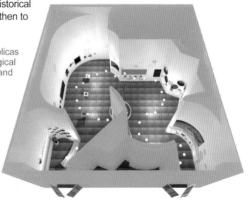

Jordan Pavilion

Theme: **"We are CITY… We are LIFE" We Make Our Ordinary Lifestyle, Extraordinary!!**

National Day: July 25

Jordan is a melting pot of cultures. The pavilion presents the charm of ancient civilization, conveys its theme, interprets the harmony between human, cities, nature and life, and delivers the idea that the development and renovation are everlasted whether in the past, present or future.

- Entrance of the pavilion resembles architectures in ancient Petra.
- The pavilion houses magnificent Khazneh. This is a grand architecture of Hellenistic style with the legend of *Ali Baba and the Forty Thieves*.
- Also displayed are the evolution of Aqaba from a port to a city of commerce and leisure, as well as the ways of living and renovation in other cities.

A Zone

Palestine Pavilion

Theme: **Olive City　Peace City**

National Day: October 16

The pavilion presents a fantastic City of Olive with a facade featuring Palestine flag and a solemn Arabic gate. In the center erects a huge olive with visual impact. Olive is important for Palestine as olive oil is the country's major product. Olive branch signifies peace and friendship, and olive green symbolizes harmony, environmental protection and sustainable development.

- On both sides and the front side inside the pavillion are two multimedia screens and a dozen of embedded lanterns displaying abundant products and distinctive culture of Palestine.
- Genuine olive oil from Palestine is sold in the showcase area.

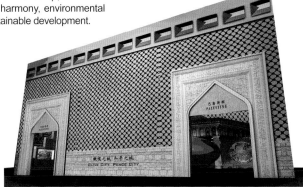

A

Zone

Syria Pavilion

Theme: **Damascus: the Oldest Capital Still Inhabited**

National Day: October 17

Distinctive architecture and culture of Syria is well interpreted by traditional elements — folk residences in Damascus dwelled by three generations. Three components of the exhibition, Cultural Stories of the Wheat/Silk Road, Arabic Library, and From Ancient Hamoukar to Modern Damascus, are respectively arranged in three halls linked with each other.

- In the courtyard there is a well in the center, valuable antiques around, and aromatic bonsais in the corners.
- Architectures and stories bring visitors to the 4 500-year history of Damascus, the capital of Syria and a city of the heaven.

Yemen Pavilion

Theme: **Yemen: Art and Civilization**

National Day: October 14

The pavilion presents Yemen's major achievements in culture, tourism, science and other sectors, stressing the importance of economy and trade in urban development. Multiple means are used to display the country's experiences in industrial development drew and borrowed from home and abroad, adapted practices in various trades on the basis of the specific local conditions, and its economic and trade prospect.

- A City Model exhibition brings scenes of modern city in Yemen; posters in Arabic, English and Chinese languages introduce historical cities, renovated villages and natural landscape of the country.
- Handicrafts and industrial products are sold in the pavilion.

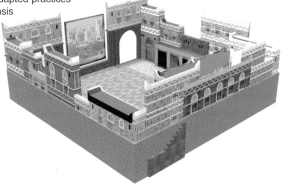

Asia Joint Pavilion III

The joint pavilion includes the exhibitions of Laos and Myanmar.

Laos Pavilion

Theme: **City of Charm — Luang Prabang
Charming World Heritage Town**

National Day: October 12

The model of Luang Prabang, a famous ancient city in Laos, together with other exhibits, displays the connection between tradition and the modern society. The exhibition highlights the interrelation between environmental protection and economic prosperity and the importance of sustainable urban development.

• The unique lamps and lanterns, textiles, handicrafts and traditional dances reflect the local customs of Laos.
• Posters and pictures show natural sceneries, such as hills, waterfalls and caves and local buildings.

Zone

Myanmar Pavilion   Theme: **Better Urbanization with Harmonized Eco-System**

National Day: June 1

The pavilion-style entrance, magnificent wall and the bridge represent distinct Southeast Asian flavor and architectural charm of Myanmar. Featuring holy temples and traditional buildings, the pavilion adopts advanced display methods to introduce local customs, rich resources and brilliant culture of Myanmar.

- Symmetrical structure and bright colors represent the architectural style of Myanmar.
- The bridge over flowing stream at the entrance reflects the country's courtyard culture.

Chinese Provinces Joint Pavilion

Like a solid platform, Chinese Provinces Joint Pavilion surrounds China Pavilion which rises at the center. A total of 31 provinces, autonomous regions and municipalities will stage their exhibitions here. They will explore the Expo theme Better City, Better Life from their own perspectives and exhibit their cultural features, city landscapes and their yearning for a better urban life.

Beijing Pavilion

Theme: Charming Capital: Culture, Technology and Environment-Friendliness

A

Theme Week: May 4−8

Zone

No single image can fully capture the immense charm of Beijing, as one of the attractions of the capital city is the dynamic changes taking place every day. That is exactly why the designers decided to make the Beijing Pavilion a building that can transform its shape alternately into the Temple of Heaven, Water Cube, NCPA, and the Bird's Nest. Within the wonderful pavilion, visitors may know more about the Hutong (lanes) that dot the city's landscape, may watch the real-time images of the Chang'an Street, and enjoy an exciting short movie directed by Zhang Yimou.

Tianjin Pavilion

Theme: The Exciting and Charming Binhai District: Eco-Friendly

Theme Week: May 9−13

The pavilion design draws inspiration from a typical western-style building in Tianjin, in an attempt to highlight the integration of Chinese and western cultures and the fascinating mix of international architectural styles that characterize the city. A high-speed train car, which is actually a small cinema, is put on display in the pavilion. There are exhibitions showing the city's unique customs and culture.

Hebei Pavilion

Theme: Charming Hebei, Beijing's Garden

Theme Week: May 14−18

The pavilion features five interconnected geometric structures surrounded by a huge glass wall. The design is inspired by the province's art of interior painting. The five buildings, like strands of DNA, form an integral "living being". They symbolize the geographic proximity and close cultural ties between Hebei and Beijing. The Chinese philosophy about integration and symbiosis runs through the exhibitions in the pavilion, which trace the history, cultural and aesthetic traditions of the province, and look into its future.

Zone

Shanxi Pavilion

Theme: **Era of Power Development**
Theme Week: May 19–23

A magnificent archway stands as the centerpiece of the pavilion design. Powdered coal bricks, an environment-friendly building material, and LED lights are used for exterior walls which show the images of the province's world cultural heritage sites, intangible cultural heritage, folk art and customs. The exhibitions in the pavilion provide a full picture of local culture, competence in energy technologies and vision for the future.

Inner Mongolia Pavilion

Theme: **Prairie Civilization in Urban Development**
Theme Week: May 24–28

The pavilion depicts a prairie civilization in urban development and manifests various elements of the prairie culture with unique exhibition items. The floor consisting of three kinds of sand manifests the Inner Mongolian people's wisdom; the contrast between the earliest nomadic habitation and modern cities shows the course of prairie city development in history; the huge tree of quicksand implies environmental changes and expresses the ideal of turning deserts into oases. Visitors can also have a virtual prairie journey on mountain bikes.

Liaoning Pavilion

Theme Week: May 29–June 2

Theme: **Liaoning: Rhythm of Steel and Sea**

The pavilion's blue metal exterior full of rhythm manifests the hardness of steel and the beauty of the sea. Above the entrance is a Sinosauropteryx model.

The exhibits include the fossils of the first bird and flower in the world, Liaoning's six world cultural heritage items and its 200 greatest contributions to China's economy; the interactive 4D cinema with 360° screen introduces the Liaoning coastal economic belt and Shenyang economic zone; multimedia movies show the charm of 14 Liaoning cities.

Jilin Pavilion

Theme: **Sing Under Changbai Mountains**

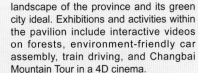

Zone

Theme Week: June 3–7

The exterior design incorporates such visual elements as Tianchi Lake of Changbai Mountain, forests and alpine gardens to exhibit the unique landscape of the province and its green city ideal. Exhibitions and activities within the pavilion include interactive videos on forests, environment-friendly car assembly, train driving, and Changbai Mountain Tour in a 4D cinema.

Heilongjiang Pavilion

Theme: **Ice and Snow Makes us Different**
Theme Week: June 8–12

The pavilion, made of crystal resin, is in the shape of an ice sculpture. Focusing on ice and snow, it displays Heilongjiang's green tourist culture and reveals its people's happy life. The interior, featuring ice, snow, water-eroded cave and other elements, makes visitors feel cool and comfortable. Visitors can see panoramic movies and folk performances riding on simulated sleds and participate in interactive games such as curling and skiing.

Jiangsu Pavilion

Theme: **Beautiful Jiangsu, Wonderful Home**
Theme Week: June 13–17

The pavilion creates a virtual garden through many high-tech means. The exterior consists of two LED screens, showing Jiangsu's openness and vitality. Main exhibition items such as Spring Flowers and Autumn Fruits, Internet of Things, Seven-colored Spectrum and Beautiful Jiangsu fully reveal Jiangsu's long history and profound culture. The development achievements of the high-tech industry represented by the Internet of things, photovoltaic and biological medicine display the essence of an ideal garden.

A

Zone

Zhejiang Pavilion

Theme: **Urban and Rural Happiness, Wonderful Home**

Theme Week: June 18−22

The pavilion's main exhibition item is designed as a huge celadon bowl brimming with water. The scenes of West Lake and Qiantang River Tide are projected onto the center of the huge bowl alternately. The four sections of High Mountains and Winding Rivers, Like a Heavenly City, Dazzling Stars and Rippling Water show Zhejiang's urbanization mode characterized by overall urban and rural planning.

Anhui Pavilion

Theme: **Hui Culture Lends Greater Charm to Life — Essential to Cities**

Theme Week: June 23−27

The pavilion focuses on the Hui culture's core idea of "openness, ambition, innovation, harmony and good faith" in urban development. The two sections of "Anhui Impression" and "Colorful Cities" depict a panoramic picture of Anhui's past, present and future. "Anhui Impression" shows calligraphic works and Anhui residences, etc. "Colorful Cities" is a multimedia presentation displaying beautiful sceneries in the province.

Fujian Pavilion

Theme: **Charming Fujian Province on the West Bank of the Strait**

Theme Week: June 28−July 2

The boat-shaped pavilion with green, blue and white as main colors fully shows the charming image of Fujian as a liveable place. Exhibits and multimedia presentation together present natural sceneries in Fujian as well as its achievements in socioeconomic development, technology and urban construction.

Jiangxi Pavilion

Theme: **Jiangxi: EcoProvince**

Theme Week: July 3–7

The pavilion, resembling a huge blue and white porcelain container, depicts the peculiar charm of Jiangxi as home to a myriad of talents and natural resources.

The exhibition presents Jiangxi's splendid scenery, profound culture and current development. The plan for the Poyang Lake Ecological Economic Zone shows that Jiangxi is pursuing sustainable development and harmony between humanity and nature.

Shandong Pavilion

Theme: **A Lush, Green Garden**
Theme Week: July 8–12

The pavilion forms the cultural conception of "stretching mountains and rivers" and depicts Shandong's geographical features from the main perspective of the towering Mt. Tai. The open entrance displays the hospitality for friends from afar. The three sections of "Wisdom Corridor", "City Window" and "Shandong Home" show Shandong's culture, charm and hospitality and future city life and express the connotation of "Harmonious but Different, Our Home".

Henan Pavilion

Theme: **Heart of the Nation, Origin of Urban Civilization**
Theme Week: July 13–17

The pavilion enumerates Henan's contributions to and impacts on the Chinese civilization, manifests the inspiration and stimulation of historical achievements for future development and reveals the harmonious future of Henan cities. It displays the long historical course of urban development. A movie on the provincial history is played in the theme cinema area, to look to the province's wonderful future.

Zone

Hubei Pavilion

Theme: **Crisscrossed by Rivers and Lakes:
A City Park**
Theme Week: July 18−22

The pavilion in the shape of the Chinese character for "water" is decorated by a phoenix pattern, a symbol unique to Hubei. It has wonderful exhibition space. Its pavilion embodies the urban development course, wonderful visions and the idea of harmony between cities and water. The main exhibition item sets forth the idea that the water history is the urban history and our history through combining the panorama screen, yarn screen and 3D ground screen system.

Hunan Pavilion

Theme: **Urban Shangri-La**
Theme Week: July 23−27

The pavilion looks like a Mobius strip. The review of Hunan's history and vision of future projected on the strip imply mankind's endless pursuit. Among sections named Nature, Future and Human Culture, the first two show the local scenery and imagine the future cities — an "urban Shangri-La" featuring ecological protection, pleasant environment, energy recycling and sustainable development; the remaining one allows children think freely about future cities in games.

Guangdong Pavilion

Theme: **Guangdong Qilou, Green Life**

Theme Week: July 28−August 1

The pavilion in the shape of Qilou (special local structure) is inspired by the local paper-cutting techniques to

demonstrate the strong Guangdong taste. The three sections of Green Life, Green Cities and Green Myths interpret the pursuit of green life through high-tech means and ingenious thoughts. The Green Myths interpreted by special-effect movies are especially moving; Brightening the Whole of Heaven shows Guangdong's beautiful green life via 3D presentation, performances and shows.

Guangxi Pavilion

Theme: **Green Home, Blue Dream**

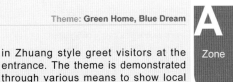

Zone

Theme Week: August 2–6

With the Elephant Trunk Mountain covered by osmanthus blossoms as visual framework, the pavilion shows the beautiful landscape. Robots dressed in Zhuang style greet visitors at the entrance. The theme is demonstrated through various means to show local customs. The bronze drum image and phantom silk ball have a unique style.

Hainan Pavilion

Theme: **Hainan: Where You Experience a Better Life**

Theme Week: August 7–11

Focusing on "vacation paradise, habitable island, open special zone", the pavilion looks magic and romantic by combining advanced digital projection technologies with wonderful silk screen designs, and makes people feel Hainan's sunshine, leisure, livability, security and other charms.

Chongqing Pavilion

Theme: **Mountains and Forest City**
Theme Week: August 12–16

The shape of the pavilion borrows the elements of Kuimen and steep mountains, highlighting the pattern of "a mountain city surrounded by two rivers". The three sections and the two interaction areas interpret the city's changes by presenting the city's footprints of ecological, cultural and urban development. The pavilion shows Chongqing's new mode of economic growth and vision of the mountains and forest city system from aspects of Habitable Chonging, Forest Chongqing, and Healthy Chongqing.

A

Zone

Sichuan Pavilion

Theme: **Water: Lifeline of Sichuan**
Theme Week: August 17—21

The two-layer structure is based on the special landscape of Sichuan. The circular wall of internal layer with 3D ecological images is encircled by the modern hyperboloid-shaped external one, embodying the harmonious coexistence of cities and nature. The history and culture of Jinsha Sunbirds lead visitors into a secluded, beautiful and harmonious world. The three sections display Sichuan's urban history and civilization, the wisdom of "following the law of nature" and wonderful future.

Guizhou Pavilion

Theme: **Guizhou: Intoxicating Beauty of a Summer Paradise**
Theme Week: August 22—26

The pavilion's grand and magnificent appearance is a combination of unique visual elements of Guizhou, such as wind and rain bridge, drum tower, etc.. The architectural shape boldly exaggerates the form of ethnic minorities' silver head decorations, displaying special folk characteristics. The pavilion shows the intoxicating beauty of local ecological environment and folk customs and the blueprint of a network city featuring harmony between man and nature.

Yunnan Pavilion

Theme: **Diverse Beauty of Yunnan:Rural-Urban Harmony**

Theme Week: August 27—31

On an open, spacious and distinctive square, Yunnan Pavilion revivifies national architectures such as Golden Horse Archway, the Bai people's residence and the Dai bamboo house, and integrates local elements like Ox-tiger Bronze Table and purple pottery from Jianshui. It presents the local "six-tier" urban system and achievements of new rural construction, and exhibits the beautiful scenery, colorful folk culture and harmonious urban-rural development on different themes via multimedia.

Tibet Pavilion

Theme Week: September 1−5

Concentrating on "New Tibet, Better Life" and taking "Environmental Protection, Folk Cultural Inheritance and Sustainable Development" as the exhibition idea, Tibet Pavilion displays the unique charms of Tibetan culture, Tibetan people's patriotism, resolution to make progress, and aspiration for well-off life, peace and harmony, through exhibited items like Qinghai-Tibet Railway, Housing Project, multimedia interactive streets and short videos.

Zone

Shaanxi Pavilion

Theme: A Cultural Trip to Chang'an
Theme Week: September 6−10

The pavilion takes the form of Tang-style palaces, and presents the living scenes of the royal family in the past and ordinary people at present, by mainly depicting the Huaqing Hot Spring, Huaqing Palace and the story in *Song of Everlasting Sorrow.* Exhibitions on four themes are held to display the splendid culture, modern urban life and natural beauty of the province, with interaction between robots and visitors, as well as wonderful folk show and Tang-style performances.

Gansu Pavilion

Theme: Silk Road, Song of Cities
Theme Week: September 11−15

Gansu Pavilion, employing LED light kit and revivified models in its exterior, demonstrates the glorious culture of Gansu Province through artistic elements of world-renowned Dunhuang Grottoes. The inside displays the vicissitudes and revival of cities along the Silk Road on three themes, and highlights Dunhuang's history and culture, urban civilization represented by the urban construction achievements since the founding of the PRC and sustainable development concept embodied by circular economy.

Zone

Qinghai Pavilion

Theme: **Source of Three Great Rivers: Watering the Nation**

Theme Week: September 16–20

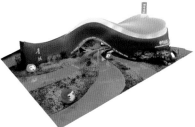

Qinghai Pavilion demonstrates how the Yantze River, the Yellow River and the Lancang River originating from Qinghai have nurtured riverfront cities and civilization, and reveals the supportive and restrictive role of the ecological conditions at the source of the three great rivers in urban development. Over ten exhibition items embrace inspiration to the public ecological concept, reflect the subsistance-development relation, and rest people's hope for ecological civilization.

Ningxia Pavilion

Theme: **Natural Ningxia, Harmonious Land**

Theme Week: September 21–25

Lumpy curves and the distinctive structure symbolize the multi-landscape and the integration of various cultures in Ningxia Province. Bearing the Islamic style, the pavilion holds exhibitions on different themes to mainly display the economic development, technical progress and culture of cities along the Yellow River, reflecting the fertility and beauty of the hinterland of the river basin and an open, harmonious and vigorous Ningxia.

Xinjiang Pavilion

Theme: **Xinjiang is a Nice Place**

Theme Week: September 26–30

With reference to Xinjiang architectural elements, the pavilion's exterior walls incorporate cultural symbols to achieve a perfect color collocation and form romantic artistic symbols. The curved lines imply the dancing silk and sand dunes. Themed as "Xinjiang is a Nice Place", the pavilion, divided in three sections, demonstrates the generosity and cheerfulness of Xinjiang people.

Shanghai Pavilion

Theme: **New Horizons Forever**

A Zone

Theme Week: October 8–12

Taking the form of Shikumen, Shanghai Pavilion features simple design but profound implication, plain appearance but modern taste, perfectly matching the city's characteristics of combination of decency and diversity, blending of history and modernism, and meeting of the East and the West. Themed as "New Horizons Forever", it demonstrates a more charming, harmonious and intelligent Shanghai through the external walls, waiting room and interior space.

Democratic People's
Republic of Korea Pavilion

Theme: **Paradise of People**

National Day: September 6

The pavilion combines traditional features and modern beauty, and adopts patterns of national flag and bronze statue of horse to decorate the exterior wall. Exhibition items such as Juche Tower, River Taedong and Korean-style arbours show Pyongyang's beautiful scenery and great achievements in various fields.

- A 4.5m-high model of Juche Tower is set in the pavilion.
- A river winds through the exhibition hall, symbolizing the River Taedong.
- A section of national customs and a small cave is set to reproduce the world heritage item (Tomb Mural) and display local paintings.

D.P.R
KOREA

A

Zone

Hong Kong Pavilion

Theme: **Hong Kong: the Infinite City**

The three-storey pavilion, with the storey in the middle transparent, reflects the modern, open and promising city, and showcases its close relationship with the world in terms of transport, information and finance.

- A miniature wetland park is set on the 3rd floor. The roofless open space guarantees sufficient sunshine and rainwater for the plants.
- Two art exhibitions will be held to introduce the development of ink-and-wash painting and the city's unique culture integrating Chinese and Western elements.

India Pavilion

Theme: **Cities of Harmony**

National Day: August 18

The pavilion's design drew inspirations from Indian's great buildings such as Siddi Syed Temple and Sanchi Stupa. Visitors will be led on a journey of Indian cities from ancient times to the present day, experiencing the life in ancient, middle-age and modern India. Themed as Cities of Harmony, its exhibition will focus on traditional culture, diverse religious beliefs, development of traditional and modern science & technology, and integration between urban and rural regions.

- Zero-chemical substances feature in the pavilion with the use of solar panels, wind power, herbs and bamboos.
- A food plaza provides traditional Indian delicacies. A shopping arcade sells a wide variety of India's local products.
- Entertainment programs from various regions of India will be staged.

Iran Pavilion

Theme: **Blending of Diverse Cultures in the City**

National Day: June 11

The pavilion depicts the dignity of Islamic architecture and the grandeur of ancient and modern Iranian art. The exhibition hall is divided into three parts concerning the history of ethnic groups and civilizations, Islamic architecture and cultural achievements. The charm of urban and rural areas as a whole is highlighted.

- As the main design element for the pavilion, water presented by audio visual effect stands for universe, soil for humanity and creation, light for nature and source of divine spirit, and colors for various species.
- Each city of Iran introduces its culture, industry history and tradition in one week.

A

Zone

Israel Pavilion

Theme: **Innovation for Life:Dialog with Nature History, and Future Needs**

National Day: May 6

The pavilion consists of two streamline buildings that resemble two clenching hands and a sea shell. Its three exhibition zones symbolize Israel's innovation and future. Visitors could "chat" with nature in Whispering Garden, learn about Jewish history in Hall of Light and enjoy 360° audio-visual performances from a floated sphere in the three-dimensional space in the Hall of Innovation, which demonstrates the technological innovations of the country.

- In the Whispering Garden, 54 tangerine trees greet visitors,displaying Israel's drip irrigation technology and agricultural features.
- Hall of Innovation showcases the modern technologies: diesel oil extraction from plants for aviation use; intelligent "horseshoes" to read the minds of the cows...
- The major exhibits include a mysterious "capsule"— a mini camera, which could be swallowed for photography, offering a pleasant physical examination.

Zone

Japan Pavilion

Theme: **Wa:Harmony of Hearts, Harmony of Arts**

National Day: June 12

Named Purple Silkworm Island, the pavilion is covered with a super-light membrane with solar cells. Special environmental technologies enable the pavilion to be an eco-friendly Breathing Organism. Assisted by scene representation and imaging technology, the structure showcases the country's visions for future urban life in 2020, the cultural origins of Japan and China, the Japanese lifestyle of living with nature, Japan's dynamic modern cities, sophisticated technologies for tackling the issues on water resources and environment, as well as civil efforts to conserve and protect nature.

- Themed as Japan-China cooperation on protection of crested ibis, the pavilion presents warming-up shows of village settings, and themed performances in traditional Japanese wooden theater.
- The warming-up shows display an amazing array of futuristic technologies such as world-class robots.
- Musical plays, which recreate the integration of Chinese Kunqu Opera and traditional Japanese Noh Drama, are staged jointly by Japanese and Chinese performers.

Kazakhstan Pavilion

Theme: **Astana – the Heart of Eurasia**

National Day: June 5

The Kazakhstan Pavilion is designed to show the youngest and dynamically developing capital of the world, Astana. The pavilion features stretched membrane and glass curtain wall, characteristic of Kazakhstan's modern architecture. The internal part of the pavilion consists of 8 areas, Territory of knowledge, 4D Cinema, Urban Matrix 2030, Interactive Entertainments, Area of Astana, Soft Tribune, Art-Zone and Farewell to Kazakhstan, illustrating the country's past, present and future.

- Visitors have a chance to know more about the young and dynamically developing capital, Astana, and its great potentials in economy and culture.
- The exhibitions use the advanced electronic and information systems to introduce visitors the customs and traditions in other cities of Kazakhstan.
- Cultural and entertaining events will be held on the National Day.

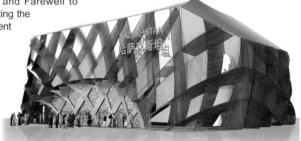

Lebanon Pavilion

Theme: **The Tell Tale Cities**

Zone

National Day: June 22

Themed on The Tell Tales Cities, the pavilion presents the true face of Lebanon — its customs and traditions, natural scenes, and historical heritage; it also tells stories about the progress of ancient cities.

- On display is the Phoenician writing on the Ahiram sarcophagus, which is widely considered to be the origin of Hebrew, Greek and Latin.
- Jeita Grotto, one of the country's natural wonders, is presented in multimedia form.
- Visitors feast their eyes on Lebanese cuisine and crafts.

Macao Pavilion

Theme: **Spirit of Cultures, Essence of Harmony**

The pavilion, in the shape of a jade rabbit lantern, is 19.99m high, implying the year of Macao's return to China. The pavilion is covered with a double-layer glass membrane and features fluorescent screens on its exterior wall.

- Two hydric balloons, as head and tail of the "rabbit", can move up and down.
- Entering the pavilion, there is a circular screen along the spiral ramp, making visitors feel like walking in a time tunnel. A movie about Macao's local customs and history is screened.

Zone

Morocco Pavilion

Theme: **Art of Living in Morocco's Urban History**

National Day: September 30

The pavilion, inspired by Morocco's rich culture, is characterized by wisdom and innovation. The three-storey building, presents the heritage of Morocco's civilization and the art of living in modern cities, expectations from urban residents and different aspects of urban life, and Morocco's reflections on history, culture, environment and urban development.

- Morocco is the only African country with a self-built pavilion, which is also the largest among the pavilions of African countries.
- The pavilion turns out to be a work of art by the choice of building materials offering a comfortable environment and the application of sophisticated audio, sound-proof, heat-proof and eco-friendly technologies.

Nepal Pavilion

Theme: **Tales of Kathmandu City: Seeking the Soul of a City; Explorations and Speculations**

National Day: September 3

The pavilion is in the form of an ancient Buddhist temple, surrounded by traditional Nepalese houses, demonstrating the architectural and artistic genius of the Nepalese architects. The pavilion demonstrates the luster of Kathmandu, the capital city of Nepal and an architectural, artistic and cultural center that has developed for over 2 000 years. The theme touches upon the soul of the city by exploring its past and future.

- The pavilion is called Araniko Center, named after a great Nepalese architect — Araniko.
- The exhibits and decorative items are all handcrafts. The exquisite patterns on the wood carvings and potteries were made by 350 Nepalese households for almost two years.
- Nepal's artists, musicians, dancers and other performers stage amazing shows.

Oman Pavilion

Theme: **Oman — An Evolving Journey**

National Day: July 22

The Oman Pavilion, shaped like an Arabian sailing boat, is an organic body consisting of buildings, roads, green system and space environment, representing the developing image of the country. A stylized glass enclosure is reminiscent of the prow of traditional Omani sailing ships, a typical scene in Oman's old capital, Nizwa and an Omani port city, Sohar. Oman shows visitors the architecture, art and culture of its ancient cities, the city of desert, the city of mountain, the offshore city, the capital city Muscat and also the blue city to be completed in 2020.

- Drawing inspiration from the story *Sinbad: Legend of the Seven Seas,* the pavilion uses videos to launch a fantastic "tour" from Sohar to Muscat and to the 2020 blue city and eventually back to Shanghai on a "magic carpet".
- Visitors can find out the country's varied terrains — sand beaches, mountain ranges, and deserts.

A Zone

Pakistan Pavilion

Theme: **Harmony in Diversity in the City**

Creating a replica of the 16th-century Lahore Fort, the Islamic-style pavilion presents the vigor and modernity of Pakistan. Visitors will be able to learn about the culture and cities of Pakistan by electronic books, its ancient civilization and religion through water curtain projection, and its streets in the theater.

- World heritage site Lahore Fort is a landmark building located in Lahore, Pakistan's cultural center.
- Pakistani clothing is exhibited. Traditional Pakistani dances are performed. A traditional restaurant serves authentical Pakistani delicacies including curry foods, BBQ, mango yogurt and milk tea, etc.

Zone

Qatar Pavilion

Theme: **Ambitions of the Present and Aspirations of the Future**

National Day: October 20

The pavilion, covered with Qatar-style patterns, is reminiscent of Barzan Tower which served as an observatory platform to chart the solar calendar as well as a beacon welcoming returning pearl divers and fishermen. A fun quiz station, Bedouin tent, special handicraft and interactive videos illustrate how the country is intent on using green technology and modern initiatives to envisage sustainable future cities.

- The Gallery within the pavilion will have regular exhibitions, including Islamic Art Museum Collection Exhibition, Egg Sculptures featuring Faberge eggs, Qatar's Stamp Exhibition and Children's Art Exhibition.
- Also on display is an underwater seascape featuring two of Qatar's important undersea resources: pearls & gas.

Republic of Korea Pavilion

Theme: **Friendly City, Colorful Life**

National Day: May 26

The exterior of the pavilion is decorated with Hangeul and art pixels. It tries to deliver a message of Communication & Integration. My City on the first floor offers a microscopic view of Seoul. The second floor, My Life, focuses on culture, technology, humanity and nature. Another exhibition area, My Dream, envisages future technologies and rehearses the 2012 Yeosu Expo.

- B Girl, Foreign Chef, Ecology Lady and IT engineer show visitors where to go.
- In My Life, visitors could understand the true face of the country: brilliant stage, houses with twittering birds and fragrant flowers, futuristic cities…

Saudi Arabia Pavilion

Theme: **Unity within Diversity**

A Zone

National Day: September 23

The pavilion, a "moon boat" elevated above the ground, features exotic Arabian gardens. Date palms are planted on the roof and the ground to provide shade. It will brief the visitors on Arabian geography, population, history, politics and highlight four types of cities: a city of energy, a city of oasis, a city of ancient culture, and a city of new economy, indicating that water, oil, and knowledge are the lifeline to Saudi Arabia.

- The pavilion, without doors and windows installed, promotes energy efficiency by utilizing the solar and wind power.
- The pavilion includes a 3D theater with a 1 600m^2 360° screen, almost the size of two football fields.

Sri Lanka Pavilion

Theme: **Tradition to Modernity**

National Day: July 18

The ceiling is decorated with traditional batik and the walls by the national flag. Five unique cities are exhibited to introduce the country's experience in heritage preservation and urban development that provides inspiration for other countries.

- Major tangible properties during urban changes are displayed via maps, models and pictures, etc.
- Besides traditional performances, Ceylon tea and spices are sold in shops.

Zone

Taiwan Pavilion

Theme: **Mountain, Water, Heart and Lantern——Nature, Soul and City**

Taiwan Pavilion, bright and beautiful, is made up of a gable-roofed building, a huge glass sky lantern and a LED sphere. The smart film covering the lantern's facade is transparent when wired up, through which visitors can see images on the LED; in case of power-off, images of local natural scenery can be projected on the facade. The display areas mainly include six sections.

- The Omnimax Theatre gives cyclic play of 4-minute movie of Natural City, and the Window of Taiwan and City Living-Room also broadcast movies.
- The sky lanterns are released in an innovative way, as people can choose blessings on the control panel of the Light-up Platform to let lanterns rise from the bottom of the LED sphere.

Turkmenistan Pavilion

National Day: May 20

The distinctive grid shape integrated with simple modern elements shows the charm of the big Central Asian country. In the interior space themed on Better City, Better Life and Oil Keeps the City Dream Alive, bright colors, brownish yellow and light gray are combined to display Turkmenistan's customs and geographical features through real objects and multimedia.

- The short video shows Turkmenistan's abundant tourist resources and tells about the story of Akhal-Teke horses. Visitors can learn more about the country's nomadic culture from the infrared touch screen.
- The pavilion displays Turkmenistan's jewels, cultural relics and exquisite carpet-making techniques through high-tech means.

UAE Pavilion

Theme: **The Power of Dreams**

A

Zone

National Day: September 27

Inspired by the precipitous sand-dunes of the UAE's legendary deserts, the pavilion recreates the changing patterns and colours of the UAE's natural and urban environments. The pavilion includes five parts. A widescreen movie entitled *In the Blink of an Eye* focuses on the great changes of living standards from the Founding of VAE to today.

- Thanks to the reflective nature of the outer covering, diffused light penetrates the building during the day and spectacularly illuminates the pavilion at night.
- Visitors are taken on a virtual journey through the UAE, as they follow "two young people" with magical powers. There is no better way to gain a bird's-eye view of the many incredible places in the country.

Uzbekistan Pavilion

Theme: **Uzbekistan: The Crossroad of Civilizations**

National Day: August 31

The exterior of the pavilion is decorated with mirror wave-like acrylic plastic which refracts the sun rays. Outside the pavilion is a sculpture of stork - the bird of happiness and prosperity and the symbol of freedom and new life. The entrance features traditional octagonal ornaments. The exhibition in the pavilion consists of six sections: The Cities Directing toward the Future, Ancient and Eternally Young Tashkent, The Cities of Progress and Creation, Harmonious City and Rural Areas. Harmony of rural area, Life Style — Traditions and the Present, Uzbekistan Is the Country of Big Tourist Potential, illustrating the

theme in various aspects.

- The section "The Cities of Progress and Creation" demonstrates the development of its numerous cities.
- The section "Uzbekistan Is the Country of Big Tourist Potential" presents Uzbekistan as a treasure house of cultural heritage, including world-renowned ancient city — Khiva.

A

Zone

Vietnam Pavilion

Theme: **The Millennium of Thang Long — Hanoi**

National Day: September 2

Re-useable bamboos as the main material reflect the cultural essence Living in Harmony with Nature. The wave-shaped exterior wall resembles a river, and bamboos help to reduce the amount of heat from sunlight. In the pavilion, visitors can perceive the country's wisdom in environmental protection and urban development.

- Events are held to celebrate the 1000th anniversary of the establishment of Hanoi.
- After the Expo, all the bamboos can be reused for welfare and school buildings.

Location Diagram of Pavilions in Zone B

Name of Restaurant

1	Colabo
2	Yicai Restaurant
3	CP Food Pavilion
4	Fresh-pure Chinese Fast-food　Cheerway
5	Zabon　Latino Restaurant
	Le Provencal-Merry Hotel　Anjile
	Relax Turkish Restaurant
6	Xiaonanguo　Food Plaza of Xinghualou Group
	Heji Xiaocai Restaurant
	Laozhengxing Restaurant
7	Deyuelou　Zhiweiguan Restaurant
	Tongqinglou Restaurant　Majesty Plaza
	Shanghai
8	Courtyard by Marriott Shanghai-Pudong
	Huatian Restaurant　Chao Food Sichuan Folk
9	Chinese Food Plaza
10	Kozuka　Shanghai Local Flavors Area

Name of Restaurant (Expo Axis)

11	B1	Christine　Wangbaohe Pudong
	B2	Caiyunjian　Mu Creative Bakery
		Croissants de France　85℃ Café　Dicos
12	01	TOT.Taste of Taiwan
	B1	Dain Ti Hill
13	B1	Burger King
14	B1	KFC　East Dawning
15	01	South Beauty
16	01	RBT Food & Beverage (Shanghai) Limited
		German Big Steak
	B1	Chamate
17	B1	Papa John's
18	01	Mister Donut　Starbucks Coffee
		Afternoon Tea
19	01	Manabe　Master Kong Chef's Table
	B1	Xinyi Restaurant
20	B2	Christine

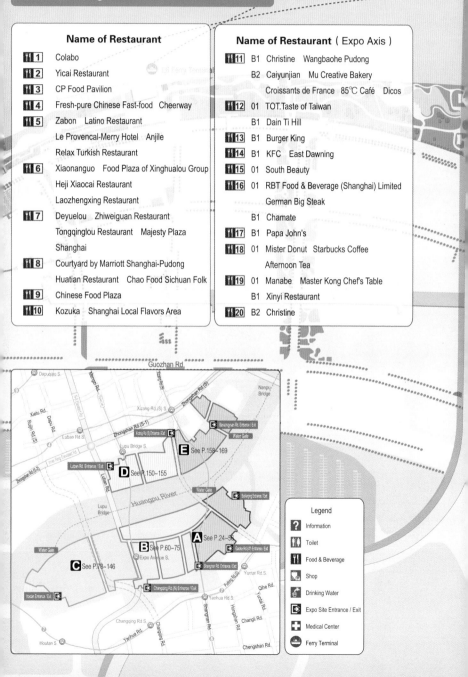

Legend

- ? Information
- Toilet
- Food & Beverage
- Shop
- Drinking Water
- Expo Site Entrance / Exit
- Medical Center
- Ferry Terminal

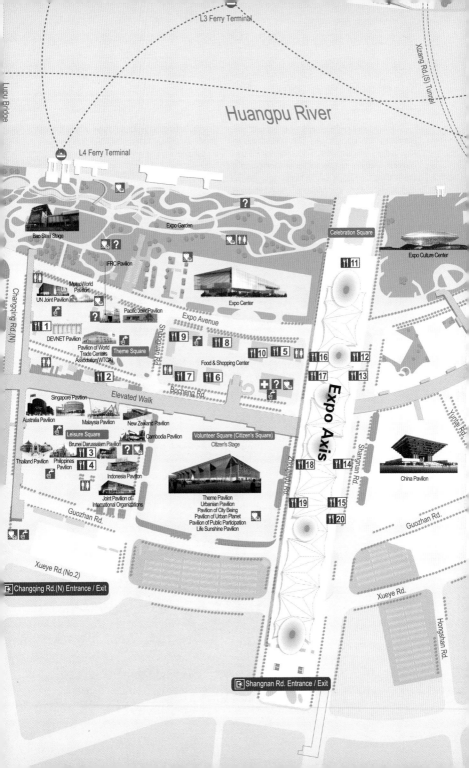

Huangpu River

L3 Ferry Terminal

L4 Ferry Terminal

Lupu Bridge

Xizang Rd.(S) Tunnel

Changqing Rd.(N)

Bao Steel Stage

Expo Garden

Celebration Square

Expo Culture Center

IFRC Pavilion

Meteo World Pavilion

UN Joint Pavilion

Pacific Joint Pavilion

Expo Center

Expo Avenue

🍴 11

DEVNET Pavilion

Theme Square

Pavilion of World Trade Centers Association(WTCA)

🍴 9

🍴 8

🍴 10

🍴 5

🍴 16

🍴 12

Food & Shopping Center

🍴 17

🍴 13

🍴 7

🍴 6

Bocheng Rd.

Shangbang Rd.

Zhoujiadu Rd.

Expo Axis

Shangnan Rd.

Yuntai Rd.

Elevated Walk

Singapore Pavilion

Australia Pavilion

Malaysia Pavilion

New Zealand Pavilion

Leisure Square

Cambodia Pavilion

Volunteer Square (Citizen's Square)

Citizen's Stage

China Pavilion

Brunei Darussalam Pavilion

🍴 3

Thailand Pavilion

Philippines Pavilion

🍴 4

Indonesia Pavilion

🍴 18

🍴 14

Joint Pavilion of International Organizations

Guozhan Rd.

Theme Pavilion
Urbanian Pavilion
Pavilion of City Being
Pavilion of Urban Planet
Pavilion of Public Participation
Life Sunshine Pavilion

🍴 19

🍴 15

🍴 20

Guozhan Rd.

Xueye Rd.(No.2)

Xueye Rd.

Hongshan Rd.

Changqing Rd.(N) Entrance / Exit

Shangnan Rd. Entrance / Exit

Australia Pavilion

Theme: **ImagiNation**

National Day: June 8

The curvy outer walls of the Australia Pavilion are sculptured like the rocks in Australia's wilderness. The exterior of the pavilion is clad in special weather-resistant steel that develops an increasingly deep, red ochre colour, evocative of the Australian outback. The pavilion comprises three parts: Journey, Discover and Enjoy, illustrating Australia's indigenous species, cultural diversity and urban livability.

- "Journey" assembles a totally-enclosed glass passage of 160 meters with six exhibition sections, displaying the history of Australia.
- "Discover" features a 1 000-seat theatre screening a multi-media show that explores the country's culture.
- Australian artists present fantastic programs.

Brunei Darussalam Pavilion

Theme: **Now... for the Future**

National Day: May 8

Tropical rainforest at the entrance shows Brunei's unique natural environment. The "ayer muleh" pattern and the height of vertical formation reflect the upturn of the living standard as well as the country's ambition to develop the economy, improve the quality of people's lives, and also the efforts to preserve natural environment, rich heritage and traditions.

- The touch screen shows the 1st National Development Plan to 2035 Blueprint.
- 4D Cinema shows wonderful scenes of Brunei through amazing audiovisual effects.
- Local food and hand woven cloth are displayed at the entrance.

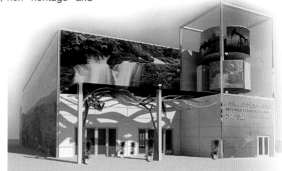

Cambodia Pavilion

Theme: **Cultural Life in the City**

National Day: June 28

The exhibition is about typical architecture of Angkor, Longvek and Phnom Penh periods which displays Cambodia's time-honored culture, art, cultural relics and rich natural resources and showcases its international awareness of protecting culture heritage.

- In Angkor Period section, visitors can see buildings made of stone in the capital of Khmer Empire such as royal monastery, temple, road, bridge, reservoir and hospital.
- In Longvek Period section, visitors can see the wide use of wood in urban construction.
- In Phnom Penh Period section, visitors can see a capital city built of cement, gravel and sand and get to know the legend about the name "Phnom Penh".

Zone

DEVNET Pavilion

Theme: **The City Rescue and Harmonious Life — Integrative International Communication & Cooperation**

Honor Day: September 8

The pavilion has a crystal clear glass facade. Its entrance is decorated with seven water-filled glass pillars that are able to display words and patterns constantly.

- A charity walk of fame is set up on the first floor to honor those giving people.

- Gold plates with 568 Chinese characters (all Chinese surnames) are exhibited on the second floor.
- On the International Gift Street, visitors are able to understand the latest development of certain world famous brands.
- On the Asian street, stone paper-making skills are displayed.

B
Zone

International Red Cross and Red Crescent Pavilion

Theme: **Humanity without Boundary**

Honor Day: May 8

The entrance of International Fedaretion of Red Cross and Red Crescent Societies Pavilion is designed as a tent, which is most commonly used in disaster relief projects, creating a sense of "being there". The pavilion is made up of three parts, showing a series of wars and other calamities that inflicted great loss and organization's unremitting endeavors in relieving human suffering.

• Each visitor is presented with a red bracelet at the entrance, delivering the message of "hearts connected".
• The theme wall captures the image of a visitor's face and red bracelet, and transmit it in real time to LCD on the wall. Visitors can see their pictures together with those of numerous volunteers.

Indonesia Pavilion

Theme: **Indonesia Bio Diver City**

A number of bamboo sticks get out from the roof of the pavilion. The pavilion is a symbol of the integration between traditional Indonesia and modern lifestyle. The four-storey building with a 600-meter passage is divided into different sections such as stage, hall, and multi-media theater. It showcases Indonesia's picturesque scenes, life of citizens as well as marine life, culture and innovation.

• The story of Zheng He's Voyages to the Western Seas is reproduced in the pavilion by a three-meter-high sculpture of Zheng He and traditional Indonesian boat.
• Indonesian songs and dances are staged every day.

Joint Pavilion of International Organizations

The joint pavilion incorporates the exhibitions of such organizations as Association of Southeast Asian Nations (ASEAN), Boao Forum for Asia (BFA), Common Market for Eastern and Southern Africa (COMESA), Le Forum Francophone des Affaires (FFA), Global Environment Facility (GEF), International Association of Public Transport (UITP), International Council of Museums (ICOM), International Network for Bamboo and Rattan (INBAR), League of Arab States, Shanghai Cooperation Organization (SCO), World Organization of United Cities and Local Governments (UCLG), World Water Council (WWC) and World Wide Fund For Nature (WWF).

B
Zone

Pavilion of Association of Southeast Asian Nations

Theme: ASEAN Community — One Vision, One Identity, One Community

Established in 1967, ASEAN is now an organization promoting cooperation in politics, economy and security in Southeast Asia. The pavilion, whose design is inspired by the beautiful winding coastlines of the region, presents the shared vision of ASEAN states to create a harmonious life.

- The pavilion provides general information on ASEAN and relevant agencies, and display photos of the member states reflecting the theme of "Better City, Better Life".
- Cultural and tourist information is displayed through posters, brochures, billboards, short movies and interactive media, familiarizing visitors with ASEAN, its culture and its traditions.

Pavilion of Boao Forum for Asia

Theme: Boao Forum for Asia — Asia, Searching for Win-Win

The blue-and-silver hue adds a modern and international element to the pavilion. The eye-catching main structure of the stand takes "ASIA" as its prototype, showing BFA's wish to bring Asian countries closer to their development goals by further regional economic integration. The logo element presented in the shape of a sphere, responding to the arc reception desk, indicates "world in union" and sheds light to the significance of "understanding, communication, win-win cooperation and building harmonious cities for a better future".

- World map as the backdrop indicates globalization, diversity and integration.
- Tropical plants and modern exhibition stand showcase the coexistence of prosperous urban economy and environment, harmony and civilization.

Pavilion of Common Market for Eastern and Southern Africa

The COMESA, with its secretariat in Lusaka, Zambia, is the largest and earliest organization established in Africa to realize economic integration by strengthening the trade and investment ties between its member states. The pavilion, including areas for exhibition and interactive activities, presents the unique charms of COMESA states, and COMESA's efforts to establish a free trade area and promote balanced socioeconomic development in its member states.

- The giant mural vividly depicts the Eastern and Southern African people's daily life.
- There are short movies on the LED screen showcasing the new faces of the member states.

Pavilion of Forum Francophone des Affaires

Theme: The City of Wonderful Life
Honor Day: June 18

Le Forum Francophone des Affaires, established in 1987 as a consortium of French-speaking enterprises, is the only non-governmental global economic organization recognized by French-speaking communities. The enclosure wall of the pavilion is built with special materials and decorated with palm trees, embodying mankind's adaptability to the environment. A big waterfall, waves between glass walls and the glazed tiles create a cool and refreshing atmosphere.

- The palace is a high-tech glass-and-steel structure, illuminated by landscape lamps and decorated by murals from across the world, combining traditional arts and modern technologies.
- A stream of water runs through a cone hung from the wood-and-brass vault and flows into a glass shell, indicating the significant role of rainwater in world ecological balance.

Pavilion of Global Environment Facility

Theme: Investing in Environmentally Friendly Technologies
Honor Day: July 20

GEF provides grants for projects related to such areas as climate change, biodiversity, international waters and the ozone layer with a view to improving global environment and promoting sustainable development of the recipients. Mainly colored green, the pavilion is designed simple but delicate.

- Visitors can learn about the history, structure and development of the GEF.
- Pictures, multi media and other means are taken to introduce the organization's contributions to experience sharing and the sound development of global environment.

Zone B

Pavilion of International Association of Public Transport

Theme: **Public Transport: Solutions for Our Future**
Honor Day: August 28

The pavilion is designed to present global public transport development, summarize experiences, and explore the potential of public transport to change cities and urban life and create a better life. Integrating green elements, it introduces the merits of public transport in a visitor-friendly, intriguing and interesting way. Visitors are to be impressed by the track and road models as well as videos and images that reflect achievements in this field.

- The history of public transport over the past 125 years is reviewed together with many best practices of public transport and interesting examples of urban planning.
- Innovative public transport elements from across the world are exhibited.
- Global participation is expected in the UITP essay contest on "Public Transport: Solutions for Our Future".

Pavilion of International Council of Museums

Theme: **Museums, Heart of the City**
Honor Day: May 18

The exhibition explores the interdependence and interaction between museums and the city in five aspects: culture, society, economy, innovation and environment. The clean, simple and modern pavilion has areas for both fixed and monthly-changing exhibitions. The front circular space can serve as both a featured exhibit area and an activity area, and the video wall at the back creates a sensational experience of modern museum environment.

- The monthly-changing exhibitions each focus on one region to present diversified images of museums.
- There are a series of activities and lectures centered on the theme, as well as special events celebrating the Honor Day.

Pavilion of International Network for Bamboo and Rattan

Theme: **Bamboo and Rattan • Human Settlements • Environment**
Honor Day: May 20

The INBAR is committed to promoting the sustainable use of bamboo and rattan. Bamboo and rattan is used to make the pavilion's exterior, interior and floor, which is eco-friendly. Various exhibits made of bamboo and rattan, such as instruments, furniture, containers and ornaments, display the important role of such materials in daily life. The exhibition also shows the organization's global network and its contributions to poverty eradication, environment protection and international cooperation.

• The short movies on the LED screen on the exterior wall present the favorable living environment created by bamboo and rattan as well as the charms of nature.

• The video column inside the pavilion is a showcase for different bamboo structures in the world and the significance of bamboo and rattan to human life.

B

Zone

Pavilion of League of Arab States

Theme: **Ancient & Modern Life of the Arab City: One Language, One Civilization, 22 Cities**

Incorporating 22 stands, the pavilion present the image of ancient and modern Arab cities and the Arabs' aspirations for the future, focusing on various aspects of life in ancient cities including culture, architecture, lifestyle, natural resources, trade and economy. It depicts the urbanization progress of 22 ancient cities and the influence of historical changes in the Arabian life.

• Posters, books, PPT presentations, movies and internet access are provided to introduce the activities of the LAS.
• A discussion Session/Lecture around "The Arab City & Urban Development" are organized.

Pavilion of Shanghai Cooperation Organization

Theme: **World Harmony Begins in the Neighborhood**
Honor Day: June 15

Here is a western-style structure inlaid with a Chinese antithetical couplet featuring the theme World Harmony Begins in the Neighborhood. Its exterior design, full of dynamism and energy, inspires imaginations of people cheerfully dancing and stepping forward to Shanghai hand by hand. Inside, the walls and the dome unfold a magnificent scene of sunrise and rosy glow, symbolizing a bright and promising future of SCO.

- The birth place of SCO — Yi Xing Pavilion of Xijiao State Guest Hotel Shanghai is presented.
- The 11.1m-long golden relief on the floor records the milestones in SCO's history and exhibits territories of its member states.

Pavilion of United Cities and Local Governments

Theme: **Men and Women for Better Cities**

Founded in May 2004, UCLG, with its secretariat in Barcelona, is known as the largest international organization of its kind. UCLG consists of governmental associations of 112 countries/regions and over 1 000 cities of 95 countries/regions.

The roofless pavilion has a reception area, an exhibition area, a recreational area and a members area. In the exhibition area 8 touch screens offer information for UCLG's 8 sections. With a touch on a city on the screen, visitors can see its home country/region highlighted on the globe. The pavilion aims to promote cooperation between UCLG members with various development phases and cultures.

- Visitors in the recreational area may interact through the screen with people online.
- The members area is used for various meetings.

B
Zone

Pavilion of World Water Council

Theme: **Water for Life and Development**
Honor Day: June 26

Better Water, Better Cities. The pavilion focuses on the role of water in creating better cities for a better life and showcases successful and innovative ways of water management for cities and citizens. It promotes the theme of Water for Life and Development and trace the life of a river from source to sea.

• Children are invited to learn about water through hands-on activities in the Kid's Corner which provides information on water challenges and solutions.
• Highlighting a variety of subjects, the exhibition focuses on challenges that various regions are facing with, such as natural disasters, the Millennium Development Goals, financing for water and climate change.

Pavilion of World Wide Fund for Nature

Theme: **River, Estuary and City**
Honor Day: June 5

The WWF, established in 1961 as an independent NGO, has gained worldwide reputation for its commitment to environment protection. Adopting Tai Chi elements, the pavilion is designed to showcase the organization's global achievements in the past 50 years, and particularly its philosophy of sustainable development of rivers, estuaries and cities against climate change. Modern interactive devices are employed to present the causes and impacts of climate change.

• Entering the "estuary", visitors can get to know the development and environment protection in such cities as Rotterdam, London, New York and Shanghai.
• The exterior and interior walls are both decorated with giant children's drawings, which well interpret the exhibition theme and depict the future life of urban in children's eyes.

B Zone

Life Sunshine Pavilion

Theme: **Eliminate Discrimination and Poverty, Cherish Life and Share Sunshine; City Offers Better Life for the Disabled**

Theme Week: May 10 — 16

As the first-ever Expo pavilion set up for the disabled, the pavilion makes the public know more about the disabled and look into their beautiful future.

• In one experience section, visitors can wear blindfolds and lean on sticks to "feel" the world, and "watch" football match with special devices.

• In another experience section, visitors can hear magic *Ode to Joy*.

• The 6th version of *My Dream* makes its debut here. Performances by the disabled and exhibitions of their calligraphic works, paintings and photos are presented.

Malaysia Pavilion

Theme: **One Malaysia — City Harmonious Living**

National Day: September 12

Composed of two gracefully sloping roofs, the pavilion resembles a sailing boat when viewed afar. Its rooftop structure is typical traditional Malaysian architecture and the sightseeing elevator draws inspiration from the Twin Towers in Kuala Lumpur. Visitors can not only appreciate the charm of the world cultural heritage sites such as Penang and Malacca, but also experience the pleasant life of an ordinary Malaysian family and watch the making of exquisite works of art.

• Its outer wall design is greatly inspired by traditional Malaysian fabric patterns, such as butterflies, flowers, birds and geometrical shapes.

• Visitors could play mini golf and traditional indoor games, experiencing truly Malaysian urban life.

• The pavilion stages two performances a day, presenting the traditional dances of 47 Malaysian ethnic groups.

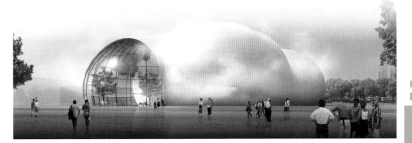

B
Zone

MeteoWorld Pavilion

Theme: For Safety and Well-being of the People

The pavilion is designed and exhibited collaboratively by World Meteorological Organization (Honor Day: May 9), European Organization for the Exploitation of Meteorological Satellites, and Group on Earth Observations.

Named White Cloud with Mist, the pavilion uses a bright white membrane structure for its exterior wall. It is composed of four white oval globes of different sizes, resembling a cloud from all perspectives. Sprayers are distributed across the membrane and could produce a misty effect when they are turned on. When the sun strikes the mist at an appropriate angle, a rainbow can be seen above the pavilion. Visitors can have a chance to experience a romantic "walk in the clouds".

- Two cartoon guiders take visitors on a wonderful "hot-air balloon ride".
- A 4-D movie tells how water droplets turn into cloud, vapor, typhoon, lightning, and rainbow.
- Celebrated weathermen from different countries are present on Honor Day.

New Zealand Pavilion

Theme: Cities of Nature: Living between Land and Sky

National Day: July 9

The wing-shaped pavilion evokes the image of land of long white clouds. Its structure encompasses cultural, scenic and humane elements, such as white clouds, gardens and natural scenes. The remarkable design of the pavilion, especially its rooftop garden, highlights the natural beauty of the country and scientific and technological innovation by its people.

- In the welcoming space, visitors can enjoy Maori dance performed by the indigenous people and to watch the Maori columns.
- A 112-meter-long multimedia corridor exhibits hundreds of pictures, displaying New Zealand's customs, geography & scenery as well as a day-in-the-life of the New Zealand family.
- The special effects team of "The Lord of the Rings" brings to life the panoramic images of New Zealand through breathtaking technologies.
- Also on display is a 1.8-ton jade boulder amazing many of the visitors.

Pacific Joint Pavilion

Theme: **Pacific — An Inspiration to Cities!**

The Pacific Joint Pavilion encompasses the exhibitions of 14 Pacific countries including Cook Islands (National Day: August 5), Fiji (National Day: August 6), Kiribati (National Day: July 12), Marshall Islands (National Day: August 17), Micronesia (National Day: August 29), Nauru (National Day: October 26), Niue (National Day: October 19), Palau (National Day: October 23), Papua New Guinea (National Day: September 17), Samoa (National Day: August 1), Solomon Islands (National Day: July 27), Tonga (National Day: August 2), Tuvalu (National Day: October 13), Vanuatu (National Day: October 8), and two international organizations including SPTO (Honor Day: May 12) and PIF (Honor Day: May 12).

The pavilion, with a plain appearance, is decorated in a unique style inside. Sixteen woven single sails, symbolizing the 16 participants, show their marvelous natural landscape, distinct cultural environment and local customs.

Pavilion of Public Participation

Theme: **Our Home**

As the only pavilion featuring public participation in the Expo Site, it highlights the idea Each Action You Take Will Change Our Life. With modern interactive methods, visitors can participate in hosting the exhibition.

- A piece of "paper" in constant change records and witnesses the urban development.
- Tens of thousands of photos display the history of world exposition, and a 4m×16m scroll adds to the magnificence.
- Visitors can take part in an interactive activity to select different sites and elements to design their ideal city.

Pavilion of World Trade Centers Association

Theme: **Peace and Stability Through Trade**

Honor Day: June 9

The pavilion exterior is gradually changed from sky blue to new grass green. The first section of the exhibition "Kaleidoscope of world trade" continuously displays videos about different WTCA member cities around the world. The second section is Around the World through World Trade Centers, enabling visitors to understand WTCA's development and history. The third section is Knowing World Trade. An interactive computer is used to interact with different WTCs.

- Visitors are presented with merchandise and handicrafts so as to get acquainted with world trade and culture of cities.
- Seminars and conferences are held and also broadcasted on the WTCA Pavilion official website in order to share the experience with people who cannot visit the pavilion in person.
- WTCA pavilion organizes a series of events and forums with themes of "Green", "IT" and "Lifestyle".

B

Zone

Philippines Pavilion

Theme: **Performing Cities**

National Day: June 9

The pavilion's exterior is covered with transparent diamond-shaped objects that can create special visual effect when wavering in the wind. The four exterior sides are decorated with catchy collages of hands. Visitors are exposed to a unique culture and performances of the country.

- TV screens at the entrance show visitors various performances of the day, and the map of the Philippines in the queuing area will highlight the tourist attractions of the country.
- Vocals, folk music, rock music, street-style performances in solo or ensemble are presented on a made-to-order stage.
- A spa experience area is opened to visitors.

B

Zone

Singapore Pavilion

Theme: **Urban Symphony**
National Day: August 7

The Singapore Pavilion looks like a huge "music box", whose sound pleases the ears of visitors even before their entry. Its exhibition sections of different shapes are linked up by gentle slopes and stairs. It integrates different design elements — music fountain, audio visual interplay and distinctive flowers on the roof garden, manifesting the harmony between cities and nature, as well as Singapore's originality and diverse cultures.

- The second floor is a pillarless exhibition hall of nearly 600 square meters. It includes three circular theaters of different sizes, showing videos of performances by Singaporean popular stars.
- The pavilion's exterior design with slots, and the cold pool around the first floor central area, serve to modulate its temperature. At night, brilliant light scatters out of the windows and slots on the outer wall, lending charm to the "music box".
- Around the pavilion, fishes move about in the cold pool, in which visitors could put their feet for "fish treatment".

Thailand Pavilion

Theme: **Thainess: Sustainable Ways of Life**
National Day: September 5

The Thailand Pavilion is designed to reflect a Thai perspective and the concept of Thainess. A palette of red and gold adorns the pavilion. Elements of Thai's traditional art and architecture and Thai lifestyle are incorporated into the pavilion. It is comprised of three exhibition halls, A Journey of Harmony, Harmony over Diversity and Happiness through Harmony. Sophisticated audio-visual technologies are employed to show Thai's history & culture and its changes that come with the globalizing currents.

- In A Journey of Harmony, visitors are transported back in time to experience the lifestyle of early Siamese. The exhibits also tells the story of the Thais' cycle of life that flourishes beside these waterways.
- Harmony over Diversity depicts the interaction between its urban and rural communities and the long-standing friendly relations between Thailand and other countries, indicating that Thai people everywhere always share a common trait: a love of peace and harmony.
- Happiness through Harmony illustrates how the Thais value a life of simplicity that follows the idea of "sufficiency" in all things they do.

UN Joint Pavilion

Theme: **One Earth, One UN**

Honor Day: October 24

The UN Joint Pavilion displays the successful practices of the UN system in such fields as sustainable development, fighting the climate change and urban management.

Participating organizations of the pavilion include FAO, IAEA, IMO, ITU (Honor Day: May 17), UNAIDS, CBD, UNFCCC, UN-HABITAT, UN (Honor Day: October 24), UNCDF, UNICEF, UNCTAD, UNESCO, UNEP, UNHCR, UNIDO, UNFPA, WB, WHO, WIPO, UNWTO and WTO.

Zone

Location Diagram of Pavilions in Zone C

Name of Restaurant

1	Haquna Matata African culture restaurant and pub
2	Burger King Papa John's
3	Pizza Hut KFC
4	Zkungfu Daniang Dumpling
5	Airest Hai Ku Japanese Restaurant
6	MX Hong Kong Yuyuan Restaurant Starbucks Coffee Manabe Harvest Festival Zhejiang Restaurant South Beauty
7	Wishdoing
8	Duck King Pleasant Turkish Restaurant
9	KFC East Dawning
10	Irish Stout
11	Uncle Fast Food Canglangting
12	Bulgarian Restaurant Tenya
13	Cel
14	Uruguay Restaurant
15	Jade Cuisine Jade Garden KFC Pizza Hut Food Plaza of Xinghualou Group Red Chicken Newcom Tea Theme Restaurant C-straits Steak/Coffee Restaurant

A See P.24~55

B See P.60~75

C See P.78~146

D See P.150~155

E See P.158~169

Houtan Entrance / Exit

Legend

?	Information
	Toilet
¶	Food & Beverage
	Shop
	Drinking Water
	Expo Site Entrance / Exit
+	Medical Center
	Ferry Terminal

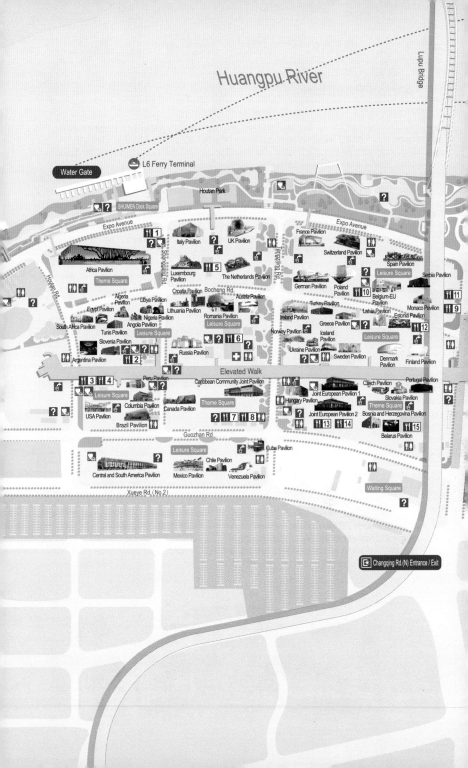

Huangpu River

Lupu Bridge

Water Gate

L6 Ferry Terminal

Houtan Park

SHUIMEN Dock Square

Expo Avenue

Expo Avenue

France Pavilion

Italy Pavilion

UK Pavilion

Switzerland Pavilion

Spain Pavilion

Serbia Pavilion

Africa Pavilion

Theme Square

Luxembourg Pavilion

The Netherlands Pavilion

German Pavilion

Poland Pavilion

Leisure Square

Belgium-EU Pavilion

Monaco Pavilion

Croatia Pavilion

Austria Pavilion

Bocheng Rd.

Turkey Pavilion

Latvia Pavilion

Estonia Pavilion

Algeria Pavilion

Libya Pavilion

Lithuania Pavilion

Romania Pavilion

Egypt Pavilion

Nigeria Pavilion

Leisure Square

Ireland Pavilion

Greece Pavilion

Leisure Square

South Africa Pavilion

Angola Pavilion

Tunis Pavilion

Leisure Square

Norway Pavilion

Iceland Pavilion

Slovenia Pavilion

Russia Pavilion

Ukraine Pavilion

Sweden Pavilion

Denmark Pavilion

Finland Pavilion

Argentina Pavilion

Elevated Walk

Peru Pavilion

Caribbean Community Joint Pavilion

Czech Pavilion

Portugal Pavilion

Leisure Square

Columbia Pavilion

Canada Pavilion

Theme Square

Hungary Pavilion

Joint European Pavilion 1

Slovakia Pavilion

Theme Square

USA Pavilion

Joint European Pavilion 2

Bosnia and Herzegovina Pavilion

Brazil Pavilion

Guozhan Rd.

Belarus Pavilion

Leisure Square

Cuba Pavilion

Central and South America Pavilion

Chile Pavilion

Mexico Pavilion

Venezuela Pavilion

Xueye Rd. (No.2)

Waiting Square

Changqing Rd.(N) Entrance / Exit

Hexing Rd.

Africa Pavilion

Africa Pavilion is the largest one among the joint pavilions in Expo 2010. It is composed of 43 independent pavilions. Forty-two countries along with the African Union organize exhibitions in the pavilion, which harbors the largest number of participants from Africa in the history of international exhibitions.

Distinctive African elements and features can be seen from the patterns on the facades. The luxuriant and gigantic tree is a symbol of the extraordinary vitality of the African Continent. The strong root stretches deep into the earth, implying that Africa is the origin of civilization. The tree absorbs nutrition from the earth through its root, so that it can reach for the sky. Likewise, Africa will become a land of hope and opportunity by drawing strength from indigenous African cultures. The desert, animals and architectures outline the diversified natural environment of the African Continent and embody the ancient yet energetic land.

There is also a public area for performance, which consists of a reality show platform, a performance stage, and an exhibition area.

African Union (AU) Pavilion

Theme: **Clean Energy for Better Management of Mega African Cities**

Honor Day: June 3

At the entrance, a gigantic African primitive sculpture with words on it echoes each other with the glimmering globe in distance, indicating how important AU is in environmental protection and coordination of world affairs. Covering subjects such as transportation, buildings & facilities, schools, etc., the pavilion illustrates the key role of clean energy plays in urban development and improving life.

- In the central round area, visitors can watch movies about urban development in Africa, particularly about environmental protection and the use of clean energy.
- Along the curving corridor, visitors can learn about the development of African countries, urban transformation, economic rise and cultural heritages in Africa.

Benin Pavilion

Theme: **Insertion of Village Territory in Cities as Engine for Sustainable Development**

Honor Day: October 6

The exterior design of the pavilion draws inspiration from the Royal Palace of Abomey and incorporates its traditional residential buildings TATA which look like chateaux. The central element of the design is the Fishing Boat, which, together with special local handicrafts and artistic decoration, helps to demonstrate the urbanization process in Benin. The pavilion is divided into two exhibition areas: the central area and the secondary area.

- The central area mainly displays the cultural attractions, traditional housing, arts and handicrafts, including bronze reliefs, wood carvings, copper sculptures and ivory carvings.
- The secondary area showcases the countryside and cities of Benin, focusing on Interaction between Rural and Urban Areas.

Botswana Pavilion

Theme: **A Heritage of Peace**

National Day: July 21

The pavilion tells about the urbanization of Botswana, attractions of this tourist country, commercial opportunities and favorable environment. Besides fascinating sceneries and abundant minerals, the country's modernization process, people's life and the influence of resources and culture on its urban development will also be introduced to visitors.

- Attractions of Botswana's landscape are showcased: vast pastures, various wildlife, the fascinating sceneries of Okavango Delta, and rich reserves of minerals.
- Visitors will find the country's heritages and arts, such as ancient buildings, stone carvings, wood carvings, paintings, music, songs and dances.

Burundi Pavilion

Theme: **Coexistence of Man and Nature**

National Day: July 3

The pavilion, emphasizing Burundi's achievements in sustainable development and economic resurrection, as well as the win-win relationship between cities (exemplified by Bujumbura) and villages, consists of a Welcome Area, Display Area that exhibits agricultural, fishery, traditional medicine and industrial products and handicrafts, Performance Area offering folklore shows, and a pub & restaurant area.

- World famous Burundian drummers and dancers in traditional costumes bring you something authentically Burundian.
- Visitors may have a taste of Burundian coffee and tea accompanied by pastries from the Lake Tanganyika area.

C
Zone

Cameroon Pavilion

Theme: **Remodeling of Communities in the City**

National Day: October 3

With a big tree as its central element and green, yellow and blue as the main color of the space, the pavilion is a reflection of the natural, optimistic and lively Cameroonian people. It simulates various natural settings like plateaus, beaches and rain forests to embody the harmony between nature and mankind. Multimedia, models and pictures are employed to show the new look of urban communities and dwellings, and to offer an interpretation of its exhibition theme.

- Dense canopy of the tree covers the whole pavilion, symbolizing the modern and romantic elements of traditional Cameroon communities and its effective protection of forests.
- The cheerful atmosphere created by the simulated football field makes people feel Cameroonian citizens' pleasures in daily life and their passions for sports, especially for football games.

Cape Verde Pavilion

Theme: Cape Verde Cities: Global and Small

National Day: July 10

The entrance simulates Cape Verde's island topography. A subsided sand table in the center displays the country's geo-landscape. The pavilion aims to show the country's history & culture, modern cities and future economic development, to showcase the wisdom of a small island country to develop in the waves of globalization.

- With simulated sound of waves and sea breeze, visitors get to know about the history of the island and feel its passion.
- Multimedia is used to display the charm of Creole Heritage and islanders' wisdom in copying with harsh environment.

C

Zone

Central African Republic Pavilion

Theme: Prosperity of Urban Economy

National Day: September 25

Central African Republic Pavilion is comprised of four areas: Entrance Area, Resources and Economy Area, Special Stage and Future Area. The pavilion showcases the country's drive for urban prosperity so as to bring a better life to its urban residents.

- In the entrance area, visitors can walk along a meandering path and watch the rare creatures of the country. With the passionate Pygmy music, they will feel the close to Central African Republic.
- In the area for displaying resources and economy, visitors will see the country's typical dwellings with dome, cotton bedding, coffee beans, precious wood furniture, handicrafts, as well as curtains and decorations inlaid with diamond.
- In the Future Area, the walls are decorated with children's smiling faces that reflect their hope for the future.

Chad Pavilion

Theme: **Cities of Plan, Cities of Harmony**

National Day: August 11

Featuring Yardang landform, the pavilion includes Entrance, Economy and Resource Area, Urban Planning Area and Interactive Area, expressing the idea of improving living conditions through harmonious development of mankind, cities and the nature. Movies, interactive multimedia, exhibits and pictures are employed to showcase the magnificent sceneries of this country and the warm-hearted people.

- The Urban Planning Area shows traditional housing and city planning in the country.
- The Economy and Resource Area introduces the petroleum-based urban development.
- Visitors will find enthralling fabrics, jewelries, household decorations and other specialties.

Comoros Pavilion

Theme: **Coexistence of Cities and Ecotourism**

National Day: July 6

Reflecting Comoros' topographical features, the pavilion includes three areas: City Area, Volcano Area and Ocean Area, respectively represented by the Old Vendredi Mosque, the Kartala Volcano, as well as the sea, coast and islands. Visitors can know about the unique species, landscapes, and civilization of this island country, as well as its people's pursuit of human-nature harmony and sustainable development.

- In the Old Vendredi Mosque, visitors will see the mysterious traditional structures and spectacular wedding ceremonies.
- The area of Kartala Volcano introduces the origin of Comoros' civilization, wildlife resources and unique topography.
- The Ocean Area shows the glorious scenery of Grande Comore, Moheli and Anjouan Islands.

Republic of the Congo Pavilion

Theme: Natural Life in the Modern Setting (Bio-Diversity, Culture, Development and Tourism)

National Day: June 16

Presenting a city with the countryside around, the pavilion has the exhibition areas for History & Culture, Economy & Natural Resources, and Art & Interaction. Through the tale of a fish saving her friend in Congo River,it aims to display the country's rich natural resources, unique biodiversity, precious historical heritages and achievements of modern development.

- The large E-book at the entrance indicates the country's stress on education.
- In History & Culture Area, the train indicates the country's running into the future, as a symbol of farewell to the past and moving towards the world.
- In the Economy & Natural Resources Area, the cargo ship indicates an open economy and a modern country.
- In the Art & Interaction Area, a simulated beach shows the country's achievements and its confidence to embrace the world.

C

Zone

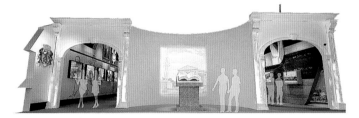

Côte d'Ivoire Pavilion   Theme: Cohabitation of Diverse Cultures in the City

National Day: August 8

The pavilion, mainly colored black, has a vinyl paint fence and mountain-shaped wall around it. Inside the pavilion, the exhibition areas are designed based on tribal dwellings, presenting a modern and traditional Côte d'Ivoire, which shares its thoughts on maintaining harmony of diversified cultures, and its opinions on keeping identity of the nation in the economic globalization.

- Tradition Area displays cases on conserving and carrying on historical heritage, stories about cultural fusion and collision, as well as tourist resources and handicrafts.
- Economy Area presents the country's current urban economy influenced by modern culture.
- Environment Area focuses on the balance between urban development and environmental protection.

Democratic Republic of the Congo Pavilion

Theme: More Harmonious and Prosperous City, More Treasures

National Day: June 23

The pavilion design presents the charm of the country in a natural and pristine environment. The main area centers on an abstract and bright-colored mine, presenting the themes of Impression and Reproduction. The secondary area focuses on Development.

- "Impression" starts from "resources" and displays the country's geo-landscape and historical background through texts, images and models.
- "Reproduction", centered on "human beings", displays real living circumstance and customs through real objects and reproduced scenes.
- "Development" displays some symbolic monuments and statues to show the course of urban development.

Djibouti Pavilion

Theme: Djibouti, Economic Hub

National Day: June 30

One end of the pavilion is "Daboita" surrounded by water and covered on top with hand-woven belts, the traditional dwelling of the nomadic Afar people, which is linked by a bridge to the other end which consists of business and leisure areas. Among others, Daboita, decorated inside with tapestries, Djibouti-style paintings, art and handicraft goods, and carpets laid on floor, focuses expressly on the local customs and practices of Djibouti, abundant tourist resources and the charming scene of the huge international habor.

- Documentaries on the Republic of Djibouti is played repeatedly on a large screen.
- People in Djibouti can see the Daboita in the pavilion and talk face-to-face with visitors in the pavilion through the Internet.

Equatorial Guinea Pavilion

Theme: **Sustainable Beauty of the City**

National Day: August 15

Three exhibition areas Seaside Scenery, Energy Exploitation and Utilization and Urban Future aim to present the shared past, present and future of nature and city, displaying how the country reaches a balance between environment and development in the process of urbanization.

- Seaside Scenery presents the statue of Saint Mary and beautiful Spanish-style architectures among coconut groves and cocoa trees.
- Energy Exploitation and Utilization displays the country's rapid economic growth driven by oil exploitation and infrastructure construction.
- Urban Future exhibits the country's bright future in industry, agriculture, tourism and education.

C
Zone

Eritrea Pavilion

Theme: **The Philosophy and Development of Urbanization in Eritrea**

National Day: May 25

The pavilion is to showcase the progress of Asmara (the city of balance) and its satellite cities in infrastructure constructions and social services. Visitors will get to know Asmara's rich cultural heritage, including Byzantine and Islamic culture and the architectures featuring modern decorative art. In the pavilion, the harmonious urban development of Eritrea will be showcased in the following four aspects: social harmony, social justice, environmental protection, and conservation and utilization of historical heritage.

- Eritrea's beautiful landscape, diversified marine life, measures on environmental improvement, archaeological discoveries, restoration of old railways, will be displayed by means of posters, slideshows, short movies, historical remains, artworks and architecture models.
- Eritrea's advanced technology in environmental protection and its relaxing, harmonious rural life will also be presented to the visitors.

Ethiopia Pavilion

Theme: **Blended Legacy of Cities: the Ethiopian Experience**

National Day: September 10

The three areas, namely, Ancient City Harar Jugol, Story of Coffee and Eight World Heritage Sites, showcase Ethiopia's civilization of centuries, wisdom and urbanization progress, as well as its inclusive manner in protecting cultural traditions and heritages and meeting urban challenges.

- In Ancient City Harar, visitors can take a walk along the streets in the ancient city, and find old buildings including the oldest mosque in Africa and the former residence of the French poet Rimbaud. The life scenes in the ancient city will be presented to visitors.
- Visitors can join in coffee parties under a huge umbrella with local features.
- There will be a breathtaking exhibition of eight world heritage sites.

C

Zone

Gabon Pavilion

Theme: **Interaction between Urban and Rural Areas**

National Day: July 30

The pavilion features red wall and wood-strip structure at the entrance, and the relief sculptures and symbols of various provinces on the facades. Three exhibition areas Rural Civilization, Urban Civilization and Natural Forestry Resources center on subjects like architecture, production, transport, culture and environment, displaying Gabon's concept of complete urban-rural integration: we come from countryside and go for cities. Explored and accomplished, we will return to the countryside.

- Rural Civilization will exhibit crafts, architectural models, photos and videos to show Gabon's rural life, particularly the evolution of its traditional residence.
- Urban Civilization will use large projections and videos to show the landscape of modern cities in Gabon.
- Natural Forestry Resources will showcase the scenery of natural reserves, animals, plants and tourism.

Gambia Pavilion

Theme: **Changing Our Cities for a Better Life**

National Day: June 15

The entrance of the pavilion is a simulation of the Arch leading to the city of Banjul. There are two areas of Natural Life and Urban Life. In order to maintain a harmonious relationship between man and nature, and realize the goal of building Gambia into an urbanized country by 2020, Gambia has laid great emphasis on the construction of infrastructures.

- Passing the arch and entering the pavilion, visitors will be impressed with the blue seawater in the center, the sailing boats, the beach chairs and umbrellas, fully exposed to the charm of this Smiling Coast of Africa.
- The area of Natural Life showcases Gambia's rich ecological resources as an ecotourism destination, and as a perfect venue to watch birds and chimpanzees.
- In the area of Urban Life, visitors can see the world-famous Juffureh Village, the statue commemorating the liberation of the serfs, and the James Island, a World Heritage Site.

Ghana Pavilion

Theme: **Garden Cities**

National Day: July 8

The pavilion is built on the basis of the iconic building in Ghana — the Gate of Freedom and Justice and traditional residential houses. The main area is to display the features of West African cities in Ghana; the secondary area is to display its unique urban development concept, namely proper use and conservation of eco-resources, and a healthy urban-rural interaction.

- Both sides of the gate are decorated with West African handcrafted carvings.
- Decorations on the facades reflect the features of traditional Ghanaian residential houses.
- An all-round image of traditional Ghana is presented to visitors through the display of holiday resorts, industrial development, herbal medicines, ethnic costumes and cloth artwork.

Guinea Pavilion

Theme: **Urban Development under Different Contexts of Environment and Natural Resources**

National Day: October 2

The pavilion is designed based on Guinean-style gatehouse. A gigantic stone column gives visitors the sense of solemnity and solidity. It will showcase its diversified natural environment and ample resources from different perspectives, and explore ways to combine resource exploitation and urban development, in a bid to promote urban development on the basis of environmental protection.

- The pavilion will make use of real objects, pictures and movies to display the culture of the four natural zones of Guinea.
- There is a dazzling array of sculptures, murals and handicrafts with distinctive folk characteristics.
- The pavilion will present by multimedia how the country tackles problems such as urban economic development, ecological conservation, migration from rural areas to cities as well as poverty issues.

C
Zone

Guinea-Bissau Pavilion

Theme: **Urbanization, Environment and Sustainable Development**

National Day: September 24

The pavilion is set in blue sky and white clouds and decorated with coconut trees. It showcases the living conditions of city dwellers of Guinea-Bissau in the past, present and future. The challenges facing the country and possible solutions will also be presented. The pavilion envisions a bright future as follows: people live in ecological, healthy, safe and livable cities, and all have access to natural resources and social services; in such a society, sustainable development will become a reality.

- In the center of the pavilion, featured performances from Guinea-Bissau will be put on stage.
- In the food section, visitors are able to savor Guinea-Bissau style cuisine while appreciating the pictures and videos about the country's culture and natural scenes.

Kenya Pavilion

Theme: Cities of Discoveries and Harmony

National Day: September 9

Four major exhibition areas of Manyatta, National Park, New City of Nairobi, and Old City of Lamu, aim to show Kenya's abundant wild animal resources, wonderful landscape, fertile land and unique urban styles, highlighting its strategy of sustainable development. The pavilion also presents the harmony between city and nature, as well as the problems in urban development.

- The Manyatta will present various Kenyan-style performances and typical daily activities in Maasai culture.

- The National Park will show how to protect wild animals in the urban development of Nairobi.
- The New City of Nairobi will present Nairobi's unique architectural elements as a regional center.
- The Old City of Lamu will present how Lamu adapts to the ever-changing external environment.

Lesotho Pavilion

Theme: Tradition and Modern Cities

National Day: October 4

A group of characteristic Basotho huts in the center of the pavilion, with stone-and-earth walls, thatch roofs, traditional kitchens and utensils inside, depict scenes of rural life and symbolise the central role of rural communities in Basotho culture. The central square is set for free communication, as to introduce the country's history, culture, economy and several ongoing projects. The integration of traditional Lesotho culture into modern cities is presented here in line with the theme.

- In the center of the hut stands a life-size sculpture of a Basotho couple in traditional costumes.
- The village huts are connected by "streams" to cities. Cultural backgrounds, history of monarchy, architectural monuments as well as cultural heritage, arts and musical instruments are presented through the display windows.

Liberia Pavilion

Theme: **A Safe City Is a Peaceful City**

National Day: August 23

The pavilion presents a nation with favorable geographical location, beautiful natural environment, and hardworking and intelligent people with the mountain-and-water setting, and water is used as a consistent element of exhibition. Three exhibition areas Liberia in Rain, People's Life and Power of Women intend to show Liberia's readiness for renaissance, happiness of regaining peace, and confidence for the future through the displayed joint efforts of the government and the people.

- Liberia in Rain displays Liberia's unique landscapes, picturesque sceneries, and its history.
- People's Life showcases how Liberian people use water effectively in daily life.
- Power of Women shows how President Ellen Johnson-Sirleaf led Liberians in ending the war and starting a new epoch in the country's history.

Zone C

Madagascar Pavilion

Theme: **Living Naturally: Diversified Ecology– Culture–Development–Tourism**

National Day: May 30

Madagascar Pavilion is dedicated to showing the country's culture, and the modernized lifestyle in cities and surrounding countryside. Entering the pavilion, visitors will be impressed by the country's distinctive landscape, the varied climate as well as the epitome of its cultural environment. The pavilion is divided into three areas: Frontal, Lateral and Pedestrian.

- A large HD screen will introduce Madagascar's national concepts to the visitors.
- The Lateral Area will demonstrate the Madagascan way of silk processing.
- In Pedestrian Area, visitors will get to the "city" from countryside in just several minutes and experience both the rural and urban life of this country.

Malawi Pavilion

Theme: **Malawi – A Smart Choice for a Better Life**

National Day: July 14

Malawi Pavilion showcases the country's experience and solutions concerning urban regeneration, cultural tradition, economic transformation, urban-rural interaction, environmental changes and urban responsibilities. When visitors enter the pavilion, they will be surrounded by the gorgeous scenery: golden beach, blue sky, serene lake and other natural views, all pristine and original. The modern civilization of cities will also be presented.

● The modern civilization is presented to the world through the exhibition of four cities, namely, Lilongwe, Blantyre, Zomba and Mzuzu. Malawi will also demonstrate its experience in protecting and improving urban environment, and in carrying on traditional heritages. Some projects for improving the social and economic life of city dwellers is also on display.

● Malawi's scenic beauty and culture are reproduced through World Heritage the Lake Malawi National Park, the Lake Malawi hailed as the most beautiful lake in central southern Africa, the traditional boat by the lake, and traditional handicrafts with African characteristics.

Zone

Mali Pavilion

Theme: **Prosperity of Urban Economy**

National Day: May 31

By adopting the colors of soil, forest and the Niger River, the pavilion exhibits totem artworks and historical architecture with Malian cultural characteristics. It showcases Mali's culture, arts, handicrafts and tourism resources, as well as the hospitality of the Malian people. The building is divided into several exhibition areas such as Art Treasures, Culture, etc.

● Inside a simulated Malian mosque, the production processes of Malian food and the culinary culture will be exhibited.
● In the Culture exhibition area, wandering among the Bogolan (a traditional Malian handicraft), the transparent blue calico and the batik fabrics, you will learn about the tourism resources and cultural essence of Mali.
● In the Art Treasures area, you will see Sudano-Sahelian buildings together with Mali's modern sculptures. Mali Pavilion will also showcase the production processes of splendid handicrafts.

Mauritania Pavilion

Theme: **Paradox between Ancient and Modern Cities of Mauritania**

National Day: July 19

The pavilion reproduces the architectures in the ancient desert city and is divided into three areas: Footprint of the Ancient City, City Impression and Urban Wisdom. It exhibits two different kinds of cities: the ancient desert city and the modern city of Nouakchott.

- In Footprint of the Ancient City, you will learn about Mauritania's ancient cities and the ancient civilizations, including architectures, environment, mode of production and the way of life.
- City Impression is devoted to displaying the image of Nouakchott as a modern city.
- In Urban Wisdom, you will see traditional tents of the desert area, and some huts from the river area. These exhibits will showcase Mauritanian people's reflection on adapting to the environment.

C
Zone

Mauritius Pavilion

Theme: **The Island City State**

National Day: May 29

The interior of the Pavilion is clad in blue and shows the physical features of the island. It is comprised of two areas: Colorful Islands and Traditional House. The pavilion will present a brand-new nation that has preserved its historical heritages and assimilated different cultures, focusing on four sub-themes: blending of diverse cultures, economic prosperity, new urban layout and technological innovation.

- Inside the pavilion, there will be an "island" to showcase Mauritius' history, bio-diversity, modern development, ship building, eco-tourism, and cultural diversity.
- In the pavilion, there is a traditional house surrounded by palm trees and sugar canes. Here visitors will experience the simple way of life in Mauritius.

Mozambique Pavilion

Theme: **Better District, Better Life**

National Day: June 25

Through exhibitions and activities, the pavilion presents Mozambique's urbanization progress and its ingenuity in achieving planned goals and sustainable growth based on regional development. It displays the distinctive sceneries and cultures of the country. The four areas, of a School, a Traditional Cottage, a Modern Residential Building and a Hospital are connected by the Zambezi River.

- Two key public projects: Armando Guebuza Bridge and Cahora Bassa Dam are exhibited.
- The Modern Residential Building, located at a corner in the front of the pavilion, is a greeting and information area, incorporating public project, urbanization, road construction and dam building.
- The School, the Hospital and the Traditional Cottage reflect the characteristic structures and relevant projects in Mozambique.

Namibia Pavilion

Theme: **Experiencing Living Diversity**

National Day: August 26

At the entrance there is an imposing elephant-shaped rock, which is flanked by a tall baobab. Focusing on the sub-themes of Exploration, Discovery and Dreams, it showcases Namibia's traditional way of life, reform of its urban community and the protection of nature and wildlife, so as to present a colorful Namibia.

- Visitors can travel through the beautiful Fish River Canyon and 11 key cities of Namibia, such as Luderitz and Swakopmund.
- A small Namibian shed is set up for visitors to have a rest and enjoy delicious local cuisine.
- In order to create a genuine Namibia atmosphere, the pavilion staff are all Namibians.

Niger Pavilion

Theme: Control of Urban Expansion and Promotion of Urban Development

National Day: August 3

Urbanization is turning Niger from an old civilization to a modern country. Its urban development concept is reflected in urban policy, urban economy and urban pattern. The pavilion, full of distinctive Nigerian characteristics, has three exhibition areas: City Pulse, Cultural Essence and Vigorous Living.

- City Pulse will present Niger's urban pattern, resources and residents to visitors, giving a full picture of Niger's urbanization.
- Cultural Essence area, featuring blue totem on white walls which is the symbol of local residence, will display cultural relics and artistic handicrafts that have witnessed Niger's 6000-year history.
- Vigorous Living will present Nigerians' daily life, agricultural production & stockbreeding as well as a variety of performances to visitors.

Rwanda Pavilion

Theme: Kigali City: Heart of Rwanda's Economic Prosperity of the Nation Reborn

National Day: July 4

Unique constructions and decorations, the new look of Kigali city and Rwandan people's endeavors to rebuild cities against many difficulties are all displayed here to offer visitors a good understanding of the accomplishments made within only 15 years and present the charm and peace of Kigali, a model city in Africa.

- Visitors can take a rest at one of the three African-styled kiosks at the center of the pavilion and get a panoramic view of the natural beauty of Kigali.
- Visitors can find a collection of local tea, coffee, handicrafts and other specialties.

Senegal Pavilion

Theme: **Infrastructure Construction, Catalyst of Sustainable and Harmonious Development**

National Day: July 24

Designed based on Senegalese map and assuming the colors of the national flag, the pavilion displays the country's infrastructures of international standards, integrated economic zones, water, forest and hygiene management as well as business cluster of tourism, handicraft and cultural industry, through such means as display walls, exhibits and multimedia. Senegal's efforts in environment protection and improvement will be fully presented.

- The majestic "lion' and the gigantic "baobab" at the entrance symbolize a country with both traditional and modern features.
- Visitors will know about a series of projects implemented in Senegal and the open and dynamic economy thereby formed.

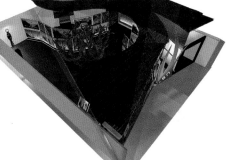

C
Zone

Seychelles Pavilion

Theme: **Sustainable Urban Development: the Seychellois Exception**

National Day: June 18

Inspired by Seychelles' natural resources and cultural features, the pavilion focuses on the country's accomplishments in keeping the harmony between nature and cities. There are three areas named Spirit of Nature, Land of Dream and Balanced City.

- The Spirit of Nature area is featured by a vast expanse of coco de mer forest, a kind of precious plant unique to Seychelles.
- The Land of Dream area displays the granite landform that exists nowhere else.
- In the Balanced City it erects a spindle-shaped column that stands for modern civilization, surrounded by spreading images of fish flocks and human smiling faces symbolizing the human-nature harmony.

Sierra Leone Pavilion

Theme: **Growth and More Urban Growth**

National Day: May 7

Mainly colored orange and decorated with huts, handmade carpets and stoneware, the pavilion gives a full African flavor. In the relaxing settings of seacoast, beach and village, the distinctive living environment in Sierra Leone is presented. The three areas, of Scenic Beauty, City Life and Urban Development showcase the country's urban development, probing into its way of building a better city.

- The Scenic Beauty area introduces the country's geological features, tourist attractions and mineral resources.
- The City Life area displays traditional living environment, folklore, handicraft and garments, accompanied with local popular music, leading visitors into Sierra Leonean people's daily life.
- Through multimedia, the Urban Development area presents rural and urban development in the country's rapid urbanization process.

Somalia Pavilion

Theme: **Boosaaso: A City with Unlimited Potential**

National Day: June 26

Featuring ample, independent yet interlinked spaces, blue-and-white tones and floating, simple lines, the mysterious and modern pavilion focuses on the city Boosaaso and its essential role in geological location and cultural exchange. It also shows the influences of different civilizations upon the urban space and lifestyle of Somalian cities, especially Boosaaso.

- Somalia's distinctive civilization, landscape, positions, beliefs, exchanges with other countries and practices of sustainable urban development are displayed clockwise.
- The "desert" area will present camel models that strongly contrast with the modern style of the pavilion.

Sudan Pavilion

Theme: **City and Peace**

National Day: July 11

Combining traditional elements and diversified forms, it presents a reserved yet fashionable image of the time-honored country. The main entrance is built like "Suakin Gate", a majestic and elegant Sudanese architecture. The three areas display Sudan's history, construction and urban development, whereby highlighting the importance of peace to the country's growth and future prosperity.

- Area I displays ancient paintings collected by Sudan Museum and introduces folk crafts, city scenery and wild animal protection in Sudan.
- Area II adopts multimedia to show the enchanting sceneries and historical progress of the country, especially the Naivasha Agreement, a milestone in Sudan's peace process.
- Areas III provides a leisure place, where you can get your finger nails painted with henna paste with blessings.

C

Zone

Togo Pavilion

Theme: **Prosperity of Urban Economy**

National Day: August 20

The pavilion showcases traditional Togolese architecture decorated with handicrafts which represent the rich culture of Togo. Three areas connected by circular corridors aim to display the development of capital city Lomé, its urban construction concept, experience in promoting urban prosperity and problems encountered in urbanization. Lomé serves as a real case on the theme.

- Handicrafts that represent the rich culture of Togo include local carpets, canvases, rural-style masks and decorative sculptures.
- On entering the pavilion, visitors can hear the beautiful music played by artists from Togo.

Uganda Pavilion

Theme: **The Philosophy and Development Urbanization in Uganda**

National Day: October 9

The three areas of Mount Ruwenzori, Lake Victoria and Kampala, representing countryside, lake area and urban community, exhibit geographical and cultural diversity, inclusive and harmonious society and sustainable environment that characterize the development of Uganda.

- Mount Ruwenzori presents the scenery of snow-capped mountains and introduces mountain gorillas, one of the local endangered species.
- In Kampala, where churches, mosques, houses and colored wall paintings depicting rural landscape are displayed, visitors can appreciate the real-life street scenes and know about public traffic, wastewater treatment, environment protection and other urban practices.

Tanzania Pavilion

Theme: **Urbanization for Sustainable Development in Tanzania: Cases of Dar-Es-Salaam and Zanzibar Cities**

National Day: July 7

The pavilion takes the color of ebony and a modernistic structure with the antique grass-stalk eaves to show the harmony between man and nature in urbanization. There is a central open area for performances and two semi-enclosed areas on both sides for exhibition. Capital city Dar-Es-Salaam and tourist resort Zanzibar are cases to display Tanzania's urban life, art and civilization, giving visitors the feeling of a harmonious melody.

- The central area features sculptures of giraffe, fantastic national parks and wildlife, and movies on Mount Kilimanjaro, the highest peak in Africa.
- Two side-areas are for folk arts and traditional wooden doors of Zanzibar Island as well as some important measures on urban development.

C
Zone

Zambia Pavilion

Theme: **Enhancing the Quality of Urban Life in Zambia**

National Day: October 24

Based on urban development practices and specific projects, the pavilion showcases Zambia's natural beauty as well as the challenges and corresponding solutions on its road of urbanization. There are three areas, namely, Victoria Falls, Town Square and Projects of Lusaka.

- On the Town Square stands a large central screen displaying the model of Lusaka, surrounded by four buildings: a redbrick dwelling house, a simple and crude residential complex, a building for commercial use and a skyscraper.

- The huge picture of the majestic and breathtaking Victoria Falls reflects the Zambezi River spirits of Zambian people.

C
Zone

Zimbabwe Pavilion

Theme: **Transforming Our Communities for a Better Life**

National Day: August 10

A simulated stone building outside the pavilion will lead visitors into the mysterious world ancient cultural relics sites of Zimbabwe. Focusing on countryside and cities and highlighting the features of the Stone City, it employs such means as posters, videos with slideshows to exhibit the country's practical wisdom and unique civilization.

- The Zimbabwean Bird standing in the center symbolizes not only the Stone City culture but also the country's accomplishments in stone carving.
- The huge light box displays the majestic Victoria Falls, embodying the Zimbabwean people's ambition to transform communities and create a better life.

Algeria Pavilion

Theme: **House of My Fathers**

National Day: July 31

The pavilion image refers to the architectural heritage of the Casbah and fully represents the traditional architectural style of North Africa and Algeria. Visitors can walk through the "street" in the pavilion while watching the short movie of *A Walk through the Casbah*, and head to the roof to experience the ancient and modern Algeria.

- Along the "street" there are arched doorways, and the large screens showing Algeria today.
- A movie is played and projected on the whole roof area, which can be watched from the top. The movie tells about the history and future of the country, embodying its determination in developing emerging cities.
- The section below the roof is highly abstract and incorporates the Algerian's imagination of the future.

Angola Pavilion

Theme: **New Angola, Bringing Better Life**

National Day: September 26

The Pavilion is beautifully decorated with African wood carvings, showcasing Angola's distinctive national features. Its exhibits include ethnic carvings and paintings. Modern exhibition technologies are employed to indicate the inseparable link between Angola and water, and present the country's efforts in sustainable urban development.

- With an aboriginal hut, visitors will be able to experience the aboriginal life of Africa by the exhibition of its primitive lifestyle.
- Through a water spray curtain, visitors could catch sight of a revolving totem, as tall as a man and all made up of leaves.

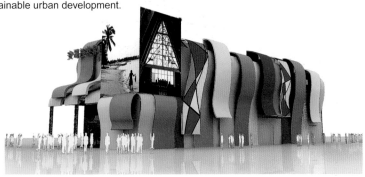

Argentina Pavilion

Theme: **Bicentennial of Argentina's Independence: A Tribute to the Achievements of its People and Cities.**

National Day: June 10

Outside the pavilion there is a green space for leisure. Inside the Pavillion, photos, traditional articles and multimedia presentations show the country's search for larger green spaces, a sustainable urbanization, the protection of historical sites and technological innovation as well as its achievements in offering a better quality of life to its urbanians.

- Exhibition shows the values of diversity: Diversity creates more experiences for tourism, more chances for investments, more knowledge for culture, and more singularity for goods and services.
- The exhibits show the Argentinean's wishes and acts in improving urban and rural life.

C

Zone

Austria Pavilion

Theme: **Austrian— Feel the Harmony**

National Day: May 21

Resembling a lying guitar, the pavilion adopts porcelain elements in its exterior walls and interior decorations, which symbolizes the return of the china exported to Europe since the Middle Ages. Roaming through the five areas, visitors will take a fantastic journey from snow-capped mountains, forests and flowing rivers to cityscape to experience the "urban-rural interaction".

- 64 projectors and millions of slides will make a feast of sensory delights. Visitors can "throw snowballs", "listen to songs of birds" and come across "squirrels" rushing under their feet.
- Visitors can enjoy the classic works by Strauss and Mozart, as well as Austrian country music, and join in avant-garde music shows and parties.
- Most of the interior walls are curved in an extremely ingenious manner.

Belarus Pavilion

Theme: Culture Diversity in the City; Economic Well-being in the City; Scientific and Technical Innovations in the City; Improvement of Living Condition; Urbanization

National Day: October 11

Multiple means will be used to show Belarus' achievements in urban development and its efforts to create a comfortable inhabitancy in cities by improving cultural diversity, economic well-being, technical innovations, living conditions and urbanization.

- Exhibition of historical and cultural heritage in Minsk, reconstructed after WWII, will show how much the capital city values peace and hates wars.
- Wildlife, eco-tourism and other exhibition items will show Belarus' experience in promoting urban-rural interaction.

Belgium-EU Pavilion

Theme of Belgium Pavilion: **Movement and Interaction**
Theme of EU Pavilion: **A European Intelligence**

National Day: June 13

The pavilion is built around the structure of a Brain Cell, evoking the artistic richness of Belgium and Europe, as well as their contributions to the development and enrichment of culture. The Brain Cell also refers directly to the role of Belgium as one of the gathering centers and cross-points of Europe's three great cultural traditions.

Belgium will hold the Presidency of the European Union in the second half of 2010. 1 000 m² of the pavilion will be offered to the EU for exhibition, presenting EU's past, present, policies and achievements.

- A dreamlike "chocolate factory" will be reproduced, in which visitors will see the process of making chocolate and even taste Belgium chocolate for free.
- Diamond designers from all over the world will bring their works to stage a top-class diamond show.

Bosnia and Herzegovina Pavilion   Theme: **Whole Country – One City**

National Day: May 9

The inner space of the pavilion is arranged in a figure "8" and multi-faceted pattern and divided into Handicraft Area, LCD and Interaction Area, Cinema and Dining Area. The country's cultural and natural diversity is presented in many aspects, displaying the balanced development of cities and villages as well as the harmonious co-existence of people with different backgrounds, which interprets the theme Whole Country – One City.

- Visitors will see artists making handicraft at the wooden handiwork bench in the central area, and they can also try making works of their own.
- In the LCD and Interaction Area, city models and multimedia movies are used to depict the image of cities in Bosnia and Herzegovina.

C

Zone

Brazil Pavilion   Theme: **Pulsing Cities: Feel the Life of Brazilian Cities**

National Day: June 3

Shaped like the "Bird's Nest", the pavilion has an exterior covered by intersecting recyclable wooden strips. The pavilion includes such exhibition sections as City Landscape, Pulsing Cities: Energetic Brazil, and Happy Brazil as well as a number of themed passages, showing the vigor of Brazilian cities through high technologies and by various cultural, artistic and commercial activities.

- Visitors will comprehend different aspects of Brazilian cities, mountains, flowers, birds and its people by the plasma display panel (PDP).
- The panoramic stage in its central exhibition hall will create an atmosphere to make visitors feel like being in a Brazilian city.
- Visitors will have the chance to meet popular Brazilian football players, who will show up in the pavilion.
- The dynamism and vitality of Brazil will also be displayed by Samba and Bossa Nova.

Canada Pavilion

Theme: **The Living City: Inclusive, Sustainable, Creative**

National Day: July 1

The pavilion is anchored by an open public place and surrounded by three large structures. It is shaped like a large letter "C", the initial of "Canada". The pavilion designates its open square as a performing area for a wide range of colorful cultural programs and highlights Canada's works of art and brilliant performances.

- Cirque du Soleil will put on spectacular acrobatics show.
- The pavilion is a showcase for Canada's rich resources and picturesque scenes. Visitors will be able to ride a bike in front of a huge three-dimensional screen, feeling as if traveling in Canada.
- The simulated waterfall will vary its flow with different movements by the visitors.

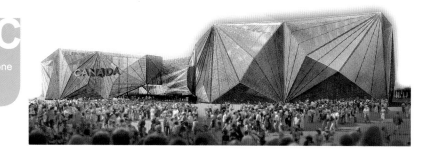

Caribbean Community Joint Pavilion

Caribbean Community Joint Pavilion encompasses the exhibitions of Antigua and Barbuda, Bahamas, Barbados, Belize, Caribbean Community, Caribbean Development Bank, Dominica, Grenada, Guyana, Haiti, Jamaica, Saint Kitts and Nevis, Saint Lucia, Saint Vincent and the Grenadines, Suriname, and Trinidad and Tobago.

Antigua and Barbuda Pavilion Theme: **The Beach Is Just the Beginning**

National Day: July 17

The pavilion, consisting of openwork roof and simple columns, is divided into Turtle Bay, Fallow Deer Drive and Black Pineapple Court. Exhibits, events and interactions introduce the culture, history and lifestyle of the country. Murals on the interior wall show the image of a developing country with noble ideals and high living standards.

- A museum of traditional Sugar Mills is set in Fallow Deer Drive to tell their history and latest development.
- Black Pineapple Court is crowded by tropical plants, and a movie tells about the country's today.

- Hawksbill Turtle is one of the national symbols. Visitors can know more about the country through touch-screen devices and take photos in the displayed costume.

C

Zone

Bahamas Pavilion

National Day: July 17

Beach mural on a partial side wall, artificial coconut trees and white sandy beach constitute a typical seascape of Bahamas. The pavilion is designed in the form of two large sailing sloops connected at the back by an open gallery and separated by a central foyer whose floor features a map of the country. Multi-faceted exhibitions will interpret fully the natural landscape, culture, and urban development of the country .

- A mural will be displayed on the wall to depict the past, present and future of capital city Nassau. A video footage of a Junkanoo Parade will also be shown.
- More images of underwater scenery, hotels, weddings, historic landmarks, etc. will be displayed on the big screen, enriching the image of Bahamas.

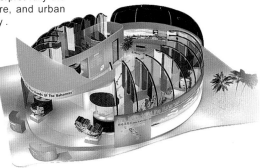

Barbados Pavilion

Theme: Blending Diverse Culture in the City

National Day: July 17

Barbados is a beautiful island-nation known as the Sanatorium of the West Indies. Various means including objects, models, and photos will be used in the exhibition to show its natural landscape, developed economy and rich culture.

- Sunshine in which Barbados is rich will be an important element of the exhibition.
- Skateboard surfing and submarine touring, most favorite among tourists, will be showcased to arouse visitors' interest in Barbados.
- Visitors will be exposed to the unique culture of Barbados as a Country of Sugar Cane.

Belize Pavilion

National Day: July 17

Belize Bluehole, one of the most fascinating destinations for diving, tells the history of Belize and will arouse the curiosity and imagination of visitors. "Palm trees" at the entrance are evocative of island landscape. The three exhibition sections — Forest Products, Mayan Relics and Marine Products, display the marvelous beach scenes, rich natural resources and unique culture.

- Belize used to be one of the main settlements for the Mayan. The specially-styled exhibition section — Mayan Relics highlights Belize's cultural traditions and carving technique.

- The Forest Products section exhibits specimens and projection of Belize's forest creatures.
- Belize's marine life and local customs are reproduced on the splendid blue background wall.

Caribbean Community Pavilion

Theme: **Many Islands, Different Experiences**

National Day: July 17

Caribbean Community (CARICOM) is a regional organization for economic cooperation whose secretariat is based in Georgetown, Guyana. The pavilion, with a special appearance and artful layout, aims to display the unique natural landscape and economic achievements of CARICOM's 15 members. A rich Caribbean ambiance is created with the exhibition of typical island scenery, a busy modern port, exquisite crafts, and children's bright smiles.

- Joyful and passionate Junkanoo parades depict the historical and cultural landscape of Bahamians.
- Straw-woven crafts will be attractive to all visitors.

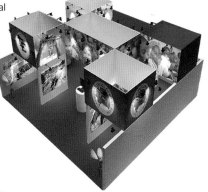

C

Zone

Caribbean Development Bank Pavilion

Theme: **Promoting A Better Life for the Caribbean People**

Honor Day: July 17

Officially founded in 1970 and headquartered in Bridgetown, capital city of Barbados, CDB facilitates coordinated economic development, cooperation and integration in Caribbean region by providing loans and assistance to the developing countries there. The pavilion with a plain style mainly showcases images and videos about the life of Caribbean people as well as the past, present and future of the Bank.

- Images in the pavilion showcase the life of common Caribbean people, and local culture.
- There are rest and business areas in the pavilion.

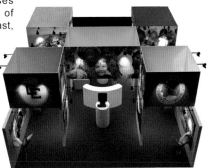

Dominica Pavilion

Theme: **Green Life in Natural Cities**

National Day: July 17

The pavilion, mainly colored green, is divided into five sections: Colorful Life, Green Power, Nation of Colors, Leisure & Rest and Business area, to display in various aspects of Dominica's development and long-term planning on use of domestic clean energy as well as its vision to improve urban and rural environment by developing green energy.

- Its open roof integrates the interior and exterior space.
- The pavilion presents Dominica's urban landscape featuring bridge, mini-windmill, cottage, etc.

Grenada Pavilion

Theme: **Rural-Urban Interaction**

National Day: July 17

In the pavilion resembling spice plant nutmeg, there are long curved viewing galleries, necessary infrastructural components and a conference area. The exhibition focuses on the urban development in the country and its experience in protecting rural tradition during urbanization.

- The display area in the red "mace petticoat" is for small chocolate products or carnival costume.
- Spice products, artwork of Caribbean style and Caribbean island scenery will be displayed.

Guyana Pavilion

Theme: One People, One Nation, One Destiny

National Day: July 17

Divided into The Time Tunnel, Guyana's Nature Wealth and Making Guyana a Modern State, the pavilion shares the country's development experience and innovative ideas, and envision urban development with visitors.

- The Time Tunnel showcases the country's abundant cultural heritage, the life of its people and its achievements in development.
- The famous Iwokrama canopy walkway, famed as Guyana's gift to the world, is the highlight of Guyana's Nature Wealth. Walking on it, visitors will fall in love with rain forest and outdoor life.

C

Zone

Haiti Pavilion

Theme: The Most Beautiful Island

National Day: July 17

The entrance of the pavilion, whose design is inspired by Haiti's topography, is a heart-shaped graffiti area representing Haitians' vision for a better life. Centering on "urban dwellers—cities—city planet", the exhibition is divided into three sections: People's Wisdom, Exotic Landscape and History & Culture.

- Visitors can draw down or write down their interpretations of Haiti on a recyclable blackboard.
- The People's Wisdom section presents Haiti's Sans Souci, Citadel and Ramiers in pictures and exhibits.
- Carnival in Jacmel, one of Haiti's most amusing cultural events, shows Haitians' passion and wisdom and tells the history of Haiti's intangible cultural heritage.

Jamaica Pavilion

National Day: July 17

Picturesque sceneries of Jamaica are ingeniously captured in the elegant pavilion with unique design. A small path winds its way and links small huts, timber gates, corridors and partitions in the exhibition area, bringing visitors into a maze. Palm trees and blooming flowers at the entrance unveil the exhibition of images, videos and models about the different aspects of Jamaica.

- Jamaica is also known as a country of Blue Mountain. Visitors here may have chance to sip the distinctive culture of Blue Mountain coffee.
- Kinston, the capital city was destroyed by earthquake in 1907 and then restored by intelligent and hardworking Jamaican people.

C

Zone

Saint Kitts and Nevis Pavilion

Theme: **Urban Cultural Heritage**

National Day: July 17

Saint Kitts and Nevis has a rich and varied culture featuring its fortresses, trains, beaches, food, etc. The pavilion is composed of four sections, i.e., World Cultural Heritage, Sugar Train, Carnival and French-style Capital, and Leisure Experience. Various means will be used to display the country's experience in urban development.

- Visitors will get to know more about Brimstone Hill Fortress National Park, one of the best preserved military buildings in Caribbean region.
- In Sugar Train section, visitors will be impressed by the narrow-gauge railway for the transport of sugar cane.
- Visitors will also be exposed to the carnival scenes in the French-style Capital Basseterre.

Saint Lucia Pavilion

National Day: July 17

The pavilion consists of local traditional buildings, particularly two with steeple tops, and large vivid pictures of island scenery. Still images and video footages will be used to depict the urban development and interaction between urbanization and tourism.

- A variety of elaborate exhibits will be used to depict people's life in Saint Lucia.
- Visitors will be exposed to the efforts in developing cities in a sustainable manner.

C Zone

Saint Vincent and the Grenadines Pavilion

Theme: **City of Arches**

National Day: July 17

The pavilion is a simulated 18th-century brick and stone building with three brick arches and two antique lampshades decorated with tropical plant patterns. Its interior, with imitation pebble flooring and simulated tropical plants, looks like a tropical forest. Galleries and video footages will be used to display the rich tourist resources of the island as an advocate of eco-tourism.

- Visitors will get to know better the culture of the country in the two galleries.
- Unique landscape of the country can be seen in photos of volcanoes, waterfalls, forests, and gardens.

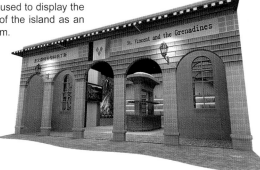

Suriname Pavilion

National Day: July 17

The pavilion is built as traditional Surinamese house and courtyard. Exhibitions about primitive Amazon rainforest, totem poles and El Dorado showcase Suriname's brilliant culture and art, picturesque natural scenery and traditional urban life with multimedia presentation and exhibits.

- The totem poles, sculpted by outstanding artists, are of distinctive Surinamese features.
- In the courtyard, statue of El Dorado is located at the end of the creek where the currents turn golden brown.

C
Zone

Trinidad and Tobago Pavilion

National Day: July 17

This is a building featuring curves: curved gates, walls and partitions in the colors of its national flag. Six areas of video display are separated by curved partitions respectively, which named after major cities of the country separately, such as Port of Spain, San Fernando and Chaguanas.

- Picturesque Caribbean island cities are shown in videos.
- The rest area provides local drinks and delicacies.

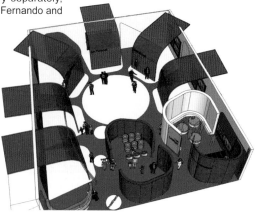

Chile Pavilion

Theme: **Relationship City**

National Day: September 18

From an aerial view, the steel-and-glass building resembles a "crystal cup" with irregular wave-like fluctuations, which is penetrated by a rectangular brown wood spiling with its end serving as the entrance to the pavilion. Composed of five exhibition halls, the pavilion focuses on Chilean understanding of the city, including how to build a better city and improve the standard of living.

- Looking into the "deep wells" in the pavilion, visitors will see images and daily lives of Chilean people on the other end of the earth.
- A seed will be found constantly changing in the "huge egg" at the center of the pavilion, symbolizing that cities' conditions could be changed.
- The U-form glass used in the pavilion allows light in but is not transparent, and provides good heat and sound insulation.

C

Zone

Columbia Pavilion

Theme: **Columbia Is Passion, the City Is Activity**

National Day: July 16

The pavilion, with a tropical flavor particularly on its exterior wall decorated with "butterflies", incorporates exhibitions on Pacific, Caribbean, Andean, Orinoco and Amazon regions. Videos, touch screens and models are used to showcase the landscape and people, natural resources and urban development of Columbia in the past, at present and in the future.

- In the Pacific Region, visitors will find themselves surrounded by the ocean, and see "cargo containers" while hearing sound of sea waves.
- In the Caribbean Region, beautiful white-sand beach and magnificent enclosing walls and castles alongside the Caribbean Sea are displayed.
- The Andean Region introduces the development of several big cities and coffee plantations in Columbia.
- The Amazon Region presents "thatched cottages", unique in Amazonian rain forest.

Croatia Pavilion

Theme: **Life is Between**

National Day: May 15

The pavilion, with its exterior colored Croatian red, has a steal-structured facade dotted by white flags flying in the air. Videos and images are shown by the 10 slide projectors on the interior side walls, displaying daily life of Croatian people in cities, urban development, differences between inland and coastal areas, and ancient and new cities.

- Visitors may listen to the sound and music of Croatian cities.
- Croatia is the origin of tie. Featured ties and shawls are sold in the souvenir shop of the pavilion.

C
Zone

Cuba Pavilion

Theme: **A City for All**

National Day: July 26

The pavilion includes an information bureau, shop, bar and other city buildings. They are of different architectural types that are integrated harmoniously; all visitors to the pavilion will feel like passing through the urban area of a town. A multi-purpose plaza serves as the center of a Cuban city, and conveys the key message that the Cuban project is based on, i.e., granting equitable opportunities to each one of its inhabitants so that they are able to participate actively in the building and transformation of the city.

- Casa del Habano presents classic Cuban cigars, tells about the history and culture of cigars, and carrys out live demonstrations.
- In Shop Cubarte, different local items are offered for sale, such as handicrafts and music CDs.
- Havana Club Bar offers for sale the typical and classic Cuban cocktails.

Czech Pavilion

Theme: **Fruits of Civilization**

National Day: May 17

The 63415 black rubber ice-hockey pucks on the white facade of the pavilion make a map of the old town of Prague. In the pavilion, on one side are the multimedia center and the theme hall which introduces Czech's solutions to city problems such as traffic jam and environment pollution, and on the other side is the main area where visitors will see a floating "city" on grassland, a virtual scenery interpreting the theme that "a city itself is a fruit of civilization".

- At the entrance is an elegantly designed spiral structure whose interior wall and floor is covered by grass. Four TV screens are installed to show the pavilion's thematic message.
- A simulated device of precipitation will lead rain water into the pavilion, showcasing recyclable use of rainwater.
- The intelligent robotic arm displayed in the pavilion can build city models with metallic materials.

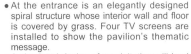

Denmark Pavilion

Theme: **Welfairytales**

National Day: June 29

The Denmark Pavilion consists of an outdoor and an indoor area which are united in two circles connected by a platform, resembling two overlapping sloping rings. It is comprised of three parts: How Do We Live, How Do We Entertain and How Do We Envisage the Future, portraying the lifestyle, characteristics and hobbies of the Danish, as well as their expectations on the future.

- The country's symbol and a world-renowned sculpture—the little Mermaid that has never left Denmark will set to make her first visit to China and greet visitors to the fairy tale world.
- Over a hundred bicycles will be available for visitors to experience Danish urban life and to understand their dreams.

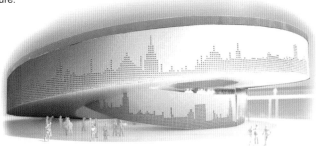

Egypt Pavilion

Theme: **Cairo, Mother of the World**

National Day: July 23

The modern-looking pavilion is mainly black and white on the exterior, and its inner space is separated by open semi-arcs, where a great number of exhibits, movies and pictures are shown to introduce Egypt's history, civilization and history-inspired response to the present and future challenges, stressing the key role of Cairo—"Mother of the World" as a cultural center of Egypt and the neighboring countries.

- Authentic antiques from Pharaonic times are displayed with slides, documentaries and music, depicting Egyptian urban life (tangible culture, folklore, rituals) and the development of Cairo.
- An inclusive Cairo will be presented in its technological, economic and social development.

C

Zone

Estonia Pavilion

Theme: **Savecity**

National Day: October 18

The colorful pavilion tells about Estonian's unique concepts and wisdom in environmental protection. "Piggy Banks", "Digital Notebook" and touchscreens are used to display Estonia's history, future, tourist sites, and business opportunities.

- Colorful and interesting Piggy Banks stand for different positive urban subjects, for example For Fresh Air, For Mobile Parking, For Green Parks.
- Visitors may send wishes to their home cities as reference for city managers in making decisions.

Europe Joint Pavilion I

Europe Joint Pavilion I will encompass the exhibitions of Cyprus, Liechtenstein, Malta and San Marino.

Cyprus Pavilion

Theme: **City of Interaction**

National Day: August 28

The pavilion, romantic and fascinating, is an epitome of the city of Cyprus. Exhibitions on the Past, the Present, the Center and Future will be presented with interactive installations, videos, pictures and exhibits to showcase the historical and cultural heritage, modern cities and future development of Cyprus as the Island of Aphrodite, highlighting its diversity, beauty, balance and modernity.

- On entering the pavilion, visitors will be deeply impressed by the huge mural of Aphrodite, glass floor with colored patterns of floral leaves as well as the feature movies projected on the wall.
- The movie *House of Aphrodite*, played repeatedly in a 3-D space, depicts a miraculous journey from the past to the future.

Liechtenstein Pavilion

Theme: **Respect and Dialogue**

National Day: September 1

Valuable cultural relics, photos and movies are used to show how the country promotes urban development and improves habitat environment at a time of urbanization and environmental degradation.

- A precious stone at the entrance area introduces the country as the Jewel of the Alps.
- 50 000 Liechtenstein postage stamps form a classical painting of the landscape around Vaduz.
- The Exhibition wall composed of dozens of large screens shows the panoramic view of the country with the help of special lighting.

C

Zone

Malta Pavilion

Theme: **Malta: 8 000 Years — A Life Center**

National Day: May 14

Different exhibition sections are connected by high-tech facilities such as intelligent lighting and audio-visual systems. Movable booths, various sculptures, giant rocks and evolution of historical cities are exhibited with sophisticated audio-visual technologies to showcase the complexity, uniqueness and development trend of Malta's modern cities.

- An audio-visual room and projectors are used to present Malta's history, resources and the dream of a better urban life.
- Exhibition highlights are shown on digital screens with light music, demonstrating the peaceful life and social harmony in Malta.

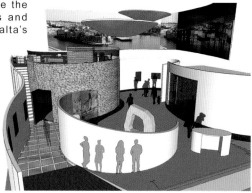

San Marino Pavilion

Theme: **The City-State**

National Day: June 4

The pavilion consists of exhibition sections on Citizens' Values, History of the Republic, Tourism, Archon, State System and Video Wall & the Earth. The charm of San Marino as a tourist destination is well reflected in the elegant porch, the replica of Statue of Liberty, corolla texture and multimedia presentations. Interactive technology and detailed information showcase the key to San Marino's rapid economic growth—high-tech industry and stable financial system.

- In the center stands a replica of the Statue of Liberty, located in Liberty Square of San Marino.

- In the virtual space of the tourism section, visitors can experience walking in the City of San Marino, capital of the Republic of San Marino which stands on Monte Titano.
- Famous performing groups from San Marino stage shows with traditional cultural features.

C

Zone

Europe Joint Pavilion II

Europe Joint Pavilion II encompasses the exhibitions of Albania, Armenia, Azerbaijan, Bulgaria, Georgia, Montenegro, Moldova and Former Yugoslav Republic of Macedonia,etc.

Albania Pavilion

National Day: May 5

Facade of the pavilion is a mottled wall resembling Albania's most ancient and characteristic city of Gjirokaster. Images of the country's landscape embedded in the archways, together with models of historical architectures and modern videos present visitors the beautiful nation of history.

- The giant hi-tech screen embedded in the huge "iceberg" throws visitors into real scenes.
- The globe-shaped projector with distinctive charm echoes delicate design idea.

Armenia Pavilion

Theme: **City of the World**

National Day: September 21

The pavilion aims to invite people of the world to construct the City of the World. Submitted models by famous architects across the world are exhibited on the booth in the middle of the pavilion to listen to opinions from all sides.

- In Apricot Garden, visitors can embrace the blossoming apricot trees, taste the unique apricots of Armenia and enjoy the magical sounds of Armenian Duduk flute made of wood from the apricot tree.
- In Gold & Silk, visitors can discover many interesting facts about ancient trade relations between Armenia and China, enjoy the unique mastery of Armenian jewelers.

Azerbaijan Pavilion

Theme: **At the Crossroads between East and West**

National Day: October 15

The Eurasian-style pavilion, colored blue, golden and white, houses exhibitions on the history, culture, and religion of cities and towns in Azerbaijan as well as the lifestyle of its urban dwellers, highlighting the important role of the country in integrating Eastern and Western cultures and in promoting the trade and communication between Eastern and Western countries.

● Exhibitions display how ancient Azerbaijan spread treasures, information, and culture between East and West through the Silk Road and its ambition to rebuild today's Silk Road.
● A general picture of today's Azerbaijan's cities and towns is depicted to show Azerbaijani ethos: cooperation with other nations and respect for each other's history, culture and belief.

C

Zone

Bulgaria Pavilion

Theme: **City of Shared Heritage**

National Day: June 14

The pavilion design is modernistic. The image of the ancient and yet modern country is depicted by linking past civilizations to present urban environment. Inside the pavilion there are two streets and a square, to showcase the transformation of the urban space during different cultural epochs. Various exhibits here offer visitors a journey through the cultural history of Bulgaria.

● Thracian gold treasures and mosaics from the Roman Empire are exhibited in the zone of Antiquity where archaeological tools are placed under the glass floor.
● The Bulgarian Revival corner, decorated like a famous museum in Bulgaria which is well-known for its amazing murals and wooden carved ceilings, features unique architectural elements such as yoke, bow windows, big eaves and close balcony.

Georgia Pavilion

National Day: October 28

The pavilion resembles a typical "courtyard" in ancient Georgian cities, in the center of which stands a giant grape "tree", symbolizing the soul of city. The four display alcoves in the museum showcase the country's historic remains, culture, natural sceneries, cities and towns, seacoast and ski resorts, interpreting the theme of Close Ties between Nature, Sceneries and Cultural Relics.

- In the Natural Scenery alcove, visitors feel like standing in a balcony overlooking the magnificent Mount Kazbek where Prometheus is said to be chained in the Greek mythology.
- Head ornaments, necklaces, crowns and bronze and iron statues made by goldsmiths in the ancient Colchis are displayed in the museum.
- Visitors can buy local handicrafts and souvenirs at the souvenir store.

Montenegro Pavilion

Theme: Montenegro: the Bridge between Civilization and Nature

National Day: May 24

The pavilion is designed based on the natural scenery of Montenegro. The exterior wall is made of perforated triangular metallic sheets that are disposed to evoke mountains. Various exhibits like forests and parks evoke the landscapes of Montenegro.

- The pavilion floor is shaped in "mountains" which go up to a point that evokes the Mount Lovcen.
- Movies and photos are used to show the scenes of the costal city Kotor.
- Unique folk dances, percussion and ballet will be staged on the National Day.

C
Zone

Moldova Pavilion

Theme: **My City Is Your City**

National Day: August 27

Themed "My City Is Your City", the pavilion presents the landscapes of hilly plains, vast prairies and dense forests in Moldova through images and videos. An inverted-pyramid with screens on each side allows visitors to enjoy different programs.

- The rest area provides elegant seats in various shapes, which are comfortable, cost-efficient and aesthetic.
- Visitors will also have chances to sip renowned Moldovan wine.

C
Zone

Pavilion of the Former Yugoslav Republic of Macedonia

Theme: **Urban Continuity**

National Day: September 7

This is an exquisite, environment-friendly structure inspired by the beehive. The interior wall is composed of numerous regular hexagons and dotted with pictures of average people's life. Images and videos bring the theme "Urban Continuity" into full play.

- The beehive structure reflects green and energy-saving awareness, as well as the vision for harmonious coexistence between all nations.
- From an ancient city to today's capital city of Macedon, historical evolution of Skopje depicts the continuity of life.

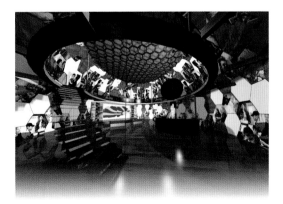

Finland Pavilion

Theme: **Well-being, Competence and the Environment**

National Day: May 27

The pavilion, Kirnu, resembles a small island surrounded by a mirror of water. Its external wall is surfaced by fishscale-like shingles. Its designer has found inspiration from nature, including small rocks found in islands, the fishscale, reflections on water, and the flavor of tar on wood. All these natural elements are reinterpreted and reproduced in the pavilion in a new way. Six elements of a better life—freedom, creation, innovation, communication, health and nature are incorporated into the building of the pavilion as well as its spatial and function design.

- The architecture is featured by the flooring of best-quality Finland wood and beautifully lit snow-cave or cloudlike structures.
- There is a Santa Claus Post Office in the pavilion. Visitors are able to meet the Santa Claus face to face and send off a Christmas card or letter bearing his signature and the mark of the Arctic Post Office.

C

Zone

France Pavilion

Theme: **The Sensual City**

National Day: June 21

Enclosed by a meshwork made of new-type concrete, the futuristic building looks like a white palace floating over a stretch of water. In the pavilion, visitors will find French delicacies, courtyards, clear water, perfumes and old movies appealing to their senses, and thereby feel the sensibility and charm of France.

- Entering the building is like stepping into an open-air French garden. The Versailles Garden, designed by French landscape architects, is full of green and rhythm.
- There is a collection of much cherished masterpieces in the Orsay Museum, including six paintings by Cezanne, Van Gogh, Miller, Manet, Bonnard and Gauguin and the sculpture The Age of Bronze by Rodin.
- At the "French Romantic Wedding", new couples take vows in the dreamy aroma of happiness.

Germany Pavilion

Theme: **balancity**

National Day: May 19

Covered with metallic silver membrane, the pavilion mainly consists of four irregular structures. Each structure is out of balance, but a stable balance is created when they interact, echoing the theme Balancity.

- Stepping into the Energy Source visitors are attracted by a large sphere covered with 400 000 LED points and showing varying images and colors. The motion of the sphere and even the images on its surface will be controlled by the audience yelling together. It displays the images of German city life and balancity. The message of the German Pavilion is that things can be moved, if people – quite literally – work together.
- Two virtual guides, Yanyan from China and Jens from Germany, introduce the exhibition to the visitors.

C

Zone

Greece Pavilion

Theme: **POLIS, the Living City**

National Day: June 19

The pavilion addresses the theme of this year's expo through a human centered approach. Polis, the Greek city constitutes "a city for living well" but also a live, a vibrant city! The design refers to the urban fabric, not as a physical replica, but as an interpretation of living and functioning in the city, as a reminder of the joy of urban life. It not only exhibits the every day way of life but also reflects an insatiable thirst for living!

- The Greece pavilion's uniqueness is that condenses 24hrs in the life of a Greek city into the 12hrs that the pavilion will be open to the public. In fact, the pavilion can be seen as a "living organism" that follows a daily cycle synchronized with the cycle of the sun in Shanghai for the duration of the Expo.
- Pavilion Halls include: Arcade, The City and The Sea, Agora, Ecologu, Urban-Rural, Theatre, Living Together, Prosperity, Promenade & Port, Square (with café-restaurant and shop).

Hungary Pavilion

Theme: **Architectural and Cultural Diversity of Our Cities**

National Day: August 22

The pavilion is a "forest" of 800 wooden sleeves which can give off light and move up and down to the music, creating superb sound and visual effects. The theme exhibition is about a homogenous object Gömböc created by Hungarian mathematicians, which makes its debut to the world. The invention, similar to the Chinese tumbler, an easily tipped toy that quickly rights itself, indicates the resoluteness and creativity of the Hungarian.

- The wooden sleeves, when pounded, can produce agreeable sounds, which would vary in the morning, the afternoon and the evening.
- A variety of Hungarian cultural events are organized on the National Day.

C

Zone

Iceland Pavilion

Theme: **Pure Energy, Healthy Living**

National Day: September 11

The Iceland Pavilion is decorated as an Ice Cube made of backlit printed fabric on the exterior. Ice patterns are visible within a "glacier". Characteristic of Iceland, the exterior walls are made of block lava to give a three-dimensional appearance. The Iceland Pavilion focuses on the relationship between Icelandic people and nature, introducing how the country has learned to use clean, renewable energy in daily life such as water power and terrestrial heat.

- Temperature in the pavilion is set at 21-22℃, and its humidity kept at a comfortable level. Fragrance from Icelandic flowers creates a sense of peace and comfort.
- Visitors are able to drink natural spring water, the purest in the world.
- Eight projectors create a 360° audio-visual effect; a video of 8-10 minutes is used to show the beautiful landscape and urban life in Iceland.

Theme: **Evolution of Urban Space and Lifestyle**

Ireland Pavilion

Theme: **Evolution of Urban Space and Lifestyle**

National Day: June 17

The pavilion consists of five cuboid exhibition areas. Connected by sloping passages and laid out at different layers, the five areas display the features of urban life in Ireland during different eras, highlighting the evolution of urban space and lifestyle along with economic and cultural development, and the efficient utilization of space and sustainable development of cities in the progress of urbanization.

- Stepping into the pavilion, visitors embark on a journey along the beautiful Liffey River, during which they come across various art galleries reconstructed from military buildings and take a sight at the urban traffic.
- Visitors can walk down the O'Connell Street, the first thoroughfare of Dublin to witness the transition of Irish cities.

C

Zone

Italy Pavilion

Theme: **City of Man**

National Day: June 2

The pavilion design is inspired by children's game Pick-up Sticks. Consisting of 20 functional modules representing a region respectively in Italy, the pavilion is like a miniature of Italian cities integrating traditional urban elements like alleys, courtyards, lanes and squares. Italy's achievements in technology, music, fashion, construction and other fields are showcased here to define a city of vigor and happiness.

- Adopting a new kind of material, transparent concrete, the pavilion features gradual change in transparency, depending on the temperature and humidity inside and outside the building.
- More than 20 units of high-tech conceptual designs are exhibited, including intelligent robots and solar cars.
- Italian tailors, blacksmiths and violin makers show their perfect crafts.

Joint Pavilion of Central and South American Countries

The joint pavilion will encompass the exhibitions of Bolivia, Costa Rica, Dominican Republic, Ecuador, El Salvador, Guatemala, Honduras, Nicaragua, Panama, Paraguay and Uruguay.

C

Zone

Bolivia Pavilion

Theme: **Urban Communities to Live Well**

National Day: August 13

Movies, interactive media, physical exhibits, and photos are displayed to interpret Bolivians' profound understanding of the concept of Beauty of Life: Flamboyance and innocence are the two sides of nature and life, which highlight the world's diversity. Exhibition sections include History, Nature, Passageway Screen, Commerce and Culture.

- In History section, three touch screens are used to display the history of Bolivia.
- In Nature section, landscaping and multimedia are used to show the eco-environment of Bolivia.
- On the circular screen, a theme movie named *I Lend You the Earth* are played.

Costa Rica Pavilion

Theme: **No Artificial Ingredients**

National Day: October 29

Costa Rica is a country in search of harmony with nature so it has identified as its objective that tourism, business, economic and social development in balance with nature. The pavilion's design is inspired by the stone sphere symbolizing the aborigines who first inhabited this land, also a cultural symbol characterizing Costa Rica. Four core themes are developed: Peace, Industry Investment, Education, and Environment.

- Visitors can taste Costa Rican food, particularly gourmet coffee, and watch the coffee making process in the pavilion.
- Cultural performances, with contemporary music concerts, art exhibitions and cocktail receptions are held.

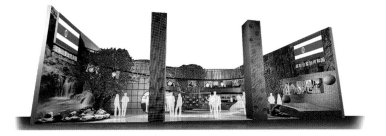

C

Zone

Dominican Republic Pavilion

Theme: **Intelligent Tropical Lifestyle**

National Day: October 5

With a long coastline and beautiful island scenery, Dominican Republic is a famous Caribbean holiday resort. The pavilion shows the country's tourism and cultural activities, its economic development, innovation and use of technology. It trys to display the relation between urbanization and the improvement of living standard and to encourage a unique and intelligent tropical lifestyle.

- The pavilion looks very European or American.
- Photos and textual information are used to present the country from different angles.

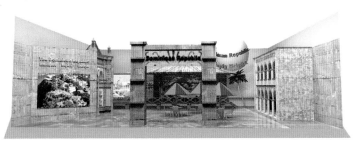

Ecuador Pavilion

Theme: **Cities and Historical Centers in Ecuador: Their Architectural Heritage and Cultural Diversity**

National Day: August 14

Design of the hemispherical dome roof is inspired by the idea of "Round Heaven and Square Earth" in traditional Chinese culture. Sections of World Center, The Islands, The Coast, The Amazon, and The Andes highlight the geographical features of Ecuador and its unique charm of cultural diversity.

- In The Islands section, visitors see through special telescopes the volcanoes and various exotic animals like giant tortoises, flamingos and lizards on the Galapagos Islands.

- Circular-screen Movies show visitors a colorful picture of a happy Ecuador.
- Visitors can experience the unique joy of participating in various folk games.

Zone

El Salvador Pavilion

Theme: **El Salvador, Country of Volcanoes**

National Day: July 20

In the pavilion's center stands a flame-blazing volcano, highlighting the primary feature of El Salvador as a country of volcanoes. Sections such as Volcano, Coffee & Crafts, and LED Screen display the country's volcano landscape, time-honored culture, use of rich geothermal and hydroelectric resources, as well as its efforts to create better life and cities.

- The huge volcano has a steel structure, with special membrane structure and chandelier in the crater reproducing a vivid scene of an erupting volcano.
- Various crafts like pottery and cotton textiles are exhibited to show the simple lifestyle that Salvadorans have inherited from Mayan culture.
- Visitors can sample and buy quality coffee nurtured in volcanic soils.

Guatemala Pavilion

Theme: **The Mayan Legacy of an Eternal Spring**

National Day: September 15

The pavilion shows the history and diversity of the Guatemalan culture and its modern urban management and pursuit of future lifestyle. The recently discovered pyramid "Mirador" is exhibited, too.

- Dance shows present how the folk art has changed through time until today.
- Cocoa, coffee, sugar and spirit drinks, which are important in the history, life and commerce of the country, are offered in the pavilion.

C

Zone

Honduras Pavilion

Theme: **We Export for Better Future**

National Day: October 27

Honduras is located in the north part of Central America. Copan, a small town in the country, is world-famous for the largest Maya Site, the religious and political center of Maya. The Pavilion in a simple and solemn style is full of Mayan elements: two stone columns at the entrance resemble the statues found in Copan, and a simulated red Mayan temple in the center bears patterns and reliefs of mysterious Mayan civilization.

- The floor is colored green and blue, symbolizing the coastal country of Honduras.
- The interior wall is sheltered by palms and bears images providing insight into the culture of the beautiful country.

Nicaragua Pavilion

National Day: September 14

The pavilion exhibits the unique natural landscapes of Nicaragua: lakes and volcanoes. The Central Stage, surrounded by water, is green on the surface, resembling a small island. The exhibition displays from a unique perspective how much Nicaraguans love life after long-standing turbulence and how much they hope to create a better life and cities for themselves and their generations.

- Simulated cascading and roaring waterfalls are presented in the Water Curtain section.
- A variety of traditional crafts and cultural events like music shows and folk dances are presented to show Nicaraguans' hospitality.

Zone

Panama Pavilion

National Day: August 16

Mainly colored blue and green, the pavilion features a simulated Panama Canal in a modern city amid blue sky and green grass. Along the canal, visitors get a general view of the ecological, geographical and cultural landscape of Panama and its efforts to build a better city.

- In Simulated Canal Lock section, a model of the reconstructed Panama Canal is presented where visitors see the opening of the canal lock and the sailing of cargo ships.
- A water-curtain molding composed of tempered glass and a water system is to show how the canal works and the importance of its connection to the Atlantic and the Pacific.
- In LED Screen section, video clips about today's Panama are played.

Uruguay Pavilion

Theme: **Quality of Life, A Commitment to Your City**

National Day: August 25

The pavilion can be imagined as a square in the city center surrounded by beautiful landscapes. Typical crafts, photos and movies are presented to display Uruguay's efforts to build modern, efficient, clean, green and friendly cities, to achieve sustainable economic and human development, and to show the quality life of its people.

- Exhibition is to show Uruguay's improvements in innovation process, wide access to internet and communications, excellent logistics infrastructure, education, energetic matrix, economic growth and equity.
- Several artistic shows are held during the Expo, with Uruguayan artists giving original performances.
- Visitors can have a rest and recreations in the Square.

C

Zone

Latvia Pavilion

Theme: **Innovation City of Science and Technology**

National Day: October 21

The pavilion, whose exterior wall features forests, sea, land, sky and wind, consists of 100 000 colourful and transparent plastic plates, which sparkle and sway in the wind. The entry stairway leads upward in a spiral, symbolizing the continued, progressive development of humanity.

- By participating in an interactive quiz using touch-screens, visitors can learn more about Latvia and may get the chance to win a flight in the vertical wind tunnel on the second floor.

Libya Pavilion

National Day: September 29

Distinctive Libyan architectures are displayed via modern exhibition means to show a city combining traditional and modern elements. The exhibits with marvelous visual effects offer visitors the original and unique experience and help them better understand the country's historical heritage and urban development.

- Large gossamer is used to simulate the changing sky from dawn to dusk in Libya.
- Narrow streets in Ghadames, scenes of Tripoli and buildings in Rome present an exotic picture.

C

Zone

Lithuania Pavilion

Theme: **Blossoming Cities**

National Day: October 25

Part of the pavilion looks like a bud just ready to burst, indicating the vitality and prosperity of the country and its cities. Exhibitions on successful cases in urban development, architectural & cultural heritage, environmental protection, sports as well as technological achievements display the harmony between man and nature when Lithuania develops into an international center of politics, culture and economy in the Baltic Sea region.

- Inside the "Bud" is an auditorium and a moving stage. Petals are made up of shells. The circular screen and surround sound can give visitors the feeling of flying above Lithuania.
- Handicraft artists give a live show of making pottery toys, crowns, wicker products, and woodcarvings. Visitors can also have a try.

Luxembourg Pavilion

Theme: **Small Is Beautiful, Too**

National Day: October 10

Inspired by the Chinese name of "Luxembourg", which literally means castle and forest, the pavilion is designed into an ancient castle carved purely out of a huge stone. It is structured as a fortress with a medieval tower in its center; its open "forest" is made up of vine gardens. Visitors will get acquainted with Luxembourg's economy, culture and lifestyle in the pavilion and appreciate the wits and creativity of its people.

- On the open wing upstairs, there is a recreation ground specially designed for children.
- In the central tower, a cultural space is designated for video communication between Shanghai and Luxembourg through satellites.
- Shanghai-themed stamps issued by Luxembourg Postal Office, and souvenir coins issued by the Central bank of Luxembourg for the Shanghai Expo, are set for sale.

C

Zone

Mexico Pavilion

Theme: **Living Better**

National Day: September 16

The pavilion features a "forest of kites" which embodies Mexico's idea of the urban life in future. The open-air green space symbolizes ecology, environment protection and peace. The three areas in the basement, at the entrance and outdoors, represent The Past, The Present and The Future of Mexico's history, culture and dreams. The outdoor green space is the center of the pavilion, echoing Mexicans' wish for more green space in cities.

- The columns of the "kites" carry numerous pores spouting cool water vapor, and are equipped with interactive touch screens showcasing sustainable development projects in Mexico.
- The pavilion displays a Mexican art collection.
- Visitors can buy or make by themselves kites and fly them on the public square.

Monaco Pavilion

Theme: **Monaco Past, Present And Future.**
The Challenges of An Evolving City-State

National Day: October 7

Several blue lighted rings of water surround the pavilion. High definition movies, old city streets with endemic flora and fauna, videos about Monaco F1 Grand-Prix and a Ferraris exhibition shed light on Monaco's cultural heritages and the progress of urban development.

- Visitors can watch a 6-minute movie *Monaco, A Rock for Eternity* in the cinema with a capacity of 250 to 300 people.

- The Sustainable Development Area demonstrates Monaco's ecological actions, while displaying an interactive terrestrial globe and an ecological concept car: the Venturi Volage!
- Visitors may take pictures in front of famous scenic spots of Monaco, and visit the info area as well as the souvenir shop which offers Monaco Grand Prix caps, golden porcelain plates, postcards, stamp collections and other interesting items.

The Netherlands Pavilion

Theme: **Happy Street**

National Day: May 18

The pavilion consists of 20 small elevated houses lining a 400m pedestrian street that curves in a figure 8 pattern. The Happy Street symbolizes an ideal city, exhibiting the rational planning of modern urban life as well as Netherlandish innovations in space, energy and water conservation.

- The winding door-less Happy Street allows for street strolls starting from any direction.
- More than perfect shelters, the fifty orange umbrellas also serve for collecting energy and converting it into electricity utilized by the pavilion.
- Exhibits in the 20 small houses can only be viewed from the outside through the windows.
- At the water purification station, visitors can get to know the purification process and have a taste of the processed water of Huangpu River.

C
Zone

Nigeria Pavilion

Theme: **Our Cities: Harmony in Diversity**

National Day: August 21

Exterior wall is a simulated Zuma Rock, known as the Gateway to Abuja, capital city of Nigeria. Color of Nigeria's national flag and simulated palm trees in the queue lobby offers a Nigerian ambiance. Three exhibition sections, i.e., Bright Star of West African Coast, Rising Country of Harmony and Business District display how to achieve the common prosperity of cities in different cultural and ethnic backgrounds.

• In Bright Star of West African Coast section, representative objects of ancient African civilizations and multimedia exhibition are presented to show Nigeria's cultural traditions. Today's Nigeria is shown in the landscaping with local tree species.

• In Rising Country of Harmony section, e-map, e-books, a large screen and a sand table are used to showcase Nigeria's diversified development at present and in the future.
• In Business District section, typical Nigerian products and cuisine are provided.

C
Zone

Norway Pavilion

Theme: **Powered by Nature**

National Day: May 28

The pavilion consists of 15 Norway "pines" and is decorated with Chinese bamboo, which presents the harmony between cities and nature, giving an interpretation of the theme "Powered by Nature". Besides Norway's varied landscapes, including the aurora, seacoast, forests, fjords and mountains, Norwegian lifestyle, urban features and the concepts of sustainable development, high energy efficiency and healthy way of living are presented.

• The giant "pines" are powered by solar energy and collected rainwater, fully embodying the idea of Sustainable Development.
• At night, the pavilion will take on colors different from those in daytime, and the fantastic scenery of aurora will unfold around visitors.
• The restaurant on the roof serves authentic Norwegian salmon and the spirits Akevitt.

Peru Pavilion

Theme: **Food Factory: Feeding the City**

National Day: July 28

For its exterior and interior decoration, the pavilion chooses bamboo and clay that have been widely used for city construction in Peru across the history. Light is let in through the woven bamboo panels. Mainly focusing on Peru's contributions to the world food industry and various local cuisines, the exhibition also highlights the process of urban evolution.

- Visitors have a chance to savor Peruvian food well known for its deliciousness and great variety.
- Videos and pictures are used to present the mysterious attractions of Peru, including the famous Inca Monument: Machu Picchu.

C

Zone

Poland Pavilion

Theme: **Poland Is Smiling**

National Day: May 22

In an abstract and irregular shape, the building is unique for its paper-cut-like surface, offering a spectacular experience to visitors as a labyrinth of light and color is formed inside the pavilion. The flexible interior space makes it possible to use the wall as a screen for movies about Polish cities. Incorporating polish people's creativity and imagination, it well interprets the theme "Poland is Smiling".

- The Chopin piano concert is held every day on the central square and in the music hall which is a tribute to the great Polish composer and pianist in the 200th anniversary of his birth.
- Every night, there are special activities for youngsters to hold parties, sometimes to Chopin's music in rock version.
- Every morning there is dragon dance show in front of the pavilion gate.

Portugal Pavilion

Theme: **Portugal, A Plaza to the World**

National Day: June 6

The pavilion's facade and interior walls are lined with cork, a recyclable, ecological material. The exhibition is organized into four sections, telling Portugal's history, culture, economy and people's life as well as the 500 years of "encounters" and history between Portugal and China.

- "Pre-Show" represents the 500 years of "encounters" and history between Portugal and China.
- The "second moment" shows a movie *Portugal, a Plaza to the World.*
- "Portugal, Energy for the World," in the "third moment" presents Portugal's endeavours in sustainable development.
- In the fourth moment, visitors arrive at a plaza called Portugal Today consisting of a cafe area, a wine tasting area, and a shop of Portuguese products.

C

Zone

Romania Pavilion

Theme: **Green City**

National Day: July 29

Also called "GREENOPOLIS", the pavilion resembles a green apple, a favorite fruit in Romania which symbolizes green city, healthy lifestyle and sustainable development. Focusing on Millennium in Retrospect, Social and Urban Development Promoted by History and Nature and City Life Close to Nature, the pavilion mainly consists of a five-storey structure with a Cultural Stage on the top that offers folklore shows, and its "sliced" areas display Romanian history, urban activities and sceneries of Bucharest.

- Visitors can enjoy such classic movies as *Stefan cel Mare* and *Mihai Viteazul* as well as modern movies that present the country's rapid growth and contemporary civilization.
- The Green Apple changes into other colors at night.
  - Collected rainwater is used to create waterfalls over the "slice". Ensconced on the roof stands, visitors can view the shows presented on the opposite open stage.

Russia Pavilion

National Day: September 28

The pavilion resembles a flower or a "tree of life", each of the 12 "petals" crowned with a tower. The white-and-golden color is turned into black-red-and-golden at night, symbolizing Russian traditional culture. The "roots" of the towers meander all the way to the "cube of civilization" on the central square and form the shape of "人" that stands for "man". The external components of the cube can be moved to create a huge "animated facade".

- Inspired by the Russian author Nosov's ideal cities, the creators of the pavilion have built a city filled with flowers accumulating solar energy, fruit-like houses and gigantic dragonfly-shaped windmills, and cars using bio fuels.
- In the central area on the first level are city layout and miniature buildings created by architects and designers from children's perspective, including flying balconies, moving houses, artificial sun, etc.
- Also on show are a lot of Russian inventions.

Serbia Pavilion

National Day: June 27

The pavilion reconstructed from a traditional Serbian building is divided into a lobby, an exhibition area and a rest area. The colorful LED points on the exterior wall makes the pavilion extremely beautiful at night. "Time" is the cohesive factor for numerous exhibits and events at the Serbian Pavilion which present the vision of better urban life and better use of time to visitors.

- Time Machine, made up of flywheels and belts, offers visitors magic experience of traveling through time.
- The Face of Serbia shows how Serbians make good use of time in urban environments.
- The Garden of Europe sums up the history of cities and the natural environment in Europe.

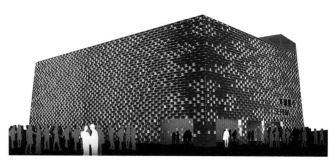

Slovakia Pavilion

Theme: **World of Humanity**

National Day: September 4

Evolution of the city is shown from the viewpoint of a square. A spiral structure of the floor presents roads of the city joining in the square.The square is surrounded by a wall with fragments of old time memories representing historical milestones in the development of Slovak towns and architecture. The movies tell city stories and the unceasing changes, movements and growth of the city.

- The disconnected curved wall represents transition from past to present and future, and also serves as a projection screen to tell a story of a city and its inhabitants.
- Visitors can be familiarized with the past ages via furniture, equipment and dress and take a picture in a historical dress.
- Famous Slovak artists bring music and dance of different genre.

C

Zone

Slovenia Pavilion

Theme: **Open Book**

National Day: June 24

Facade of the pavilion is an attractive "book shelf" with more than 1 000 books on it. The eight huge "books" in the pavilion echo "eight immortals crossing the sea" in the Chinese culture and show Slovenia's economy, culture, technology, nature, and sports. Visitors travel from the symbol of knowledge and appreciate the perfect whole of scenery, creatures and culture in the country.

- Visitors can "read" each book through audio-visual means and wall-projection.
- By seeing projections and experiencing the sounds, temperatures and even smells, the eight "books" leave visitors differentiated dreamlike impressions.

South Africa Pavilion Theme: The Rise of a Modern Economy – Ke Nako!

National Day: August 9

The concrete archway binds the simple and chaste pavilion under a huge "umbrella". The bright colors in the pavilion represent the diverse cultures of South Africa and show it as an emerging country with a vision to create better life for its people.

- Each South African iconic image recessed into the framework is accentuated by a halo effect, and the Zebra printed ottomans in the seating area enhance South Africa's aspects of nature.
- A full color screen is applied around the outer central core to project images, sounds and features of authentic South African culture.
- An "atrium" is created in the pavilion which is dressed with circular ostrich leather ottomans encompassed within wooden beams, representing a traditional "Kraal" boma enclosure.

C

Zone

Spain Pavilion Theme: From the City of Our Parents to the City of Our Children

National Day: August 30

The Spain Pavilion is designed to be a hand-weaved wicker basket structure supported by the steel framework inside. Sunlight traverses the interstices between wicker boards on the interior of the streamlined pavilion. It is comprised of three exhibition halls: Origin, City and Children. Visitors feel as if walking on a Spanish city street, marveled at the glorious past of the country as well as the wits and creativity of its people. Besides, they have a chance to feast their eyes on what excellent Spanish urban planners, sociologists,

filmmakers and artists have prepared for them.

- 8524 wicker boards of different colors decorates the exterior wall of the pavilion; ancient Chinese characters are pieced together using wicker to present a Chinese poem.
- The renowned flamenco dances are staged by Spanish performers.
- A restaurant that could accommodate 300 people, serves the most authentically Spanish cuisine.

Sweden Pavilion

Theme: **Spirit of Innovation**

National Day: May 23

The pavilion consists of four parts connected by elevated corridors, resembling the cross on Swedish national flag. It is decorated with meshwork outside and natural elements inside, symbolizing cities and the nature. Its exhibitions focus on sustainable development, innovation and communication, and showcase in detail Sweden's solutions to challenges and its measures and capacities for urban environment improvement, and underline the importance of enhancing communication in an era of new technologies.

- If unfolded, the exterior wall of the pavilion is an artistically rendered map of downtown Stockholm.
- The well-known fairy tale figure "Pippi Longstocking", as one of the guides, leads visitors into an amazing tour of innovation.
- Visitors can learn more about the Nobel Prize.
- On the top-floor terrace where Swedish coffee and circus performances are offered, visitors can interact with street artists, or buy Swedish souvenirs.

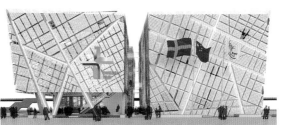

C

Zone

Swiss Pavilion

Theme: **Rural - Urban Interaction**

National Day: August 12

The urban setting on the ground floor is counterbalanced by the natural space on the roof and the continuous circuit of the chair lift provides easy access to the rural and urban areas, offering an interesting and inspiring experience. The architecture embodies the symbiosis between town and country, and emphasizes the perfect balance among man, nature and technology.

- Visitors can take the cable car from the urban environment up to the relaxing rural setting on the roof.
- The interactive, intelligent facade enveloping the pavilion is triggered by light energy in the surroundings, resulting in a haphazard pattern of flashes.
- Some Swiss people can be seen on 12 large life-size screens against the background of the Alps, talking about their visions of the future.
- Visitors may also enjoy the IMAX movie *The Alps*.

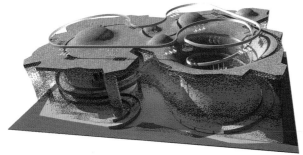

Tunisia Pavilion

Theme: **Enthusiastic City, Connected City**

National Day: September 19

The pavilion features symmetric archway, European-styled castle and flower patterns. The grating plates on the side elevation well present different images of traditional and modern cities in Tunis. Exhibition is divided into three sections of Country of Magnificent Sceneries, City of Diversified Cultures and Capital of Time-honored Civilization.

- Visitors see the "blue-and-white town" and traditional garden courtyard with local features, and learn about Tunisian traditional music and fragrance products.
- In the café, visitors can taste and make Tunisian handmade coffee.
- In the amphi-theatre, whose interior, exterior and seats are all designed based on the Roman relics most famous in Tunis, movies of its sceneries, culture and civilization are played.

C
Zone

Turkey Pavilion

Theme: **The Cradle of Civilizations**

National Day: June 20

Inspired by one of the first known settlements in the world, Çatalhöyük in Anatolia, the pavilion's two layers of exterior walls are decorated with ancient mural paintings and frescos. Its exhibition is divided into three parts: Dreaming of the Past, Cultivating the Present and Aspiring to the Future. The multilayered stories of the past are fragmented into the snapshots of images and objects. The visitors are led into "a maze of dreams".

- The center of the Pavilion presents a 360 degree movie, to establish a link between the two mega-cities: Istanbul and Shanghai. The content creates the illusion of flying, swimming and actually walking on the streets of Istanbul.
- There are a series of splendid cultural events, including folk music and ballet shows, the Fashion Show—Traditional Clothes of "Anatolian Civilizations", and the Janissary Band.

Ukraine Pavilion

Theme: **From the Ancient to Modern City**

National Day: August 24

Trigram-like wall decorations in red, black and white originate from the symbol of an ancient tribe. Snake symbolizes passage of time and change of seasons. Dog means the force to drive away the evil and Sun is a symbol of endless power. The exhibition focuses on the theme to show Ukraine's past farming culture, today's modern culture and its future urban architecture.

- Carpathian State National Park, Europe's largest national forest park and one of Ukraine's seven natural wonders, is exhibited to show Ukraine's efforts to increase the vitality of eco-environment in cities.
- Folkloric performances and live shows of traditional processes of making ceramics, embroidery and woodcuts are presented. Visitors can also try making color eggs or pottery jars in the pavilion.

C
Zone

UK Pavilion

Theme: **Building on the Past, Shaping Our Future**

National Day: September 8

The Seed Cathedral, centerpiece of the pavilion, is covered by 60 000 crystalline spines that are tipped with tiny lights. They illuminate the pavilion during the day and make the whole structure glitter at night. The journey through the UK Pavilion, which is separated into several parts: Green City, Open City, Seed Cathedral, Living City and Open Park, encourages visitors to pay attention to the role of nature and wonder how to meet the social, economic and environmental challenges of our cities.

- Green City presents the urban landscape of the four UK provincial capitals. The UK has a rich tradition of incorporating green spaces and water into its cities.
- Seed Cathedral exhibits seeds of different shapes and types from Kew's Millennium Seed Bank collection.
- Living City displays real and imaginary plants.

US Pavilion

Theme: **Rising to the Challenge**

National Day: July 2

Designed and built with a waterfall media wall and an ecological roof garden, the pavilion deals with the theme Rising to the Challenge from four aspects, namely, Sustainable Development, Teamwork Spirit, Healthy Life and Achievements of Chinese Americans, presenting the country's culture, values, innovation spirit and business success.

- Through multimedia technologies, the pavilion tells a story about an ordinary American's view of innovation and sustainable development, in which a Chinese American youth will lead the visitors into a future space.
- The exhibition on achievements of Chinese Americans includes a wall erected in recognition of the outstanding contributions made by Chinese Americans in the fields of science, culture, politics, commerce and social service.

C

Zone

Venezuela Pavilion

Theme: **Better Life, Better City**

National Day: July 5

The pavilion assumes the shape of "Mobius strip", which leads to a 3D pattern known as "Klein Bottle", i.e. a boundless and continuous curved surface where the inside mixes with the outside, symbolizing that a city resembles an eternal path-way. A fusion of characteristic elements such as open-air courtyard, ascending steps, living space of indigenous inhabitants and Bolivar Square presents Venezuelan culture, art and lifestyle.

- There is no obvious outside-inside boundary, so that visitors might find themselves step outside the pavilion just after turning around a corner.
- Several symphony concerts are staged in the music hall, including the performance of Simón Bolívar Youth Symphony Orchestra. Movies, videos and other multi-media programs are offered.

Location Diagram of Pavilions in Zone D

Name of Restaurant

⑪1 Pizza Hut   KFC

⑪2 Hongchangxing(Muslim)
Bao Steel Hotel Restaurant   Wafumura
Shendacheng Restaurant   Wumi Porridge
South Beauty   Zagara   Jade Garden
Dinglianfang

⑪3 Yungho Soybean Restaurant   Hanamaru

⑪4 Wufangzhai   Laofengge   Pinzhenxuan

⑪5 Osaka·Sakai's Pu
Ming Hong-Tangyang Congou Black Tea

⑪6 Zkungfu   Yinuo Coffee   Lihua Fast Food

⑪7 Jiji Town   Hesheng Tea Banquet
Asahibeer Restaurant

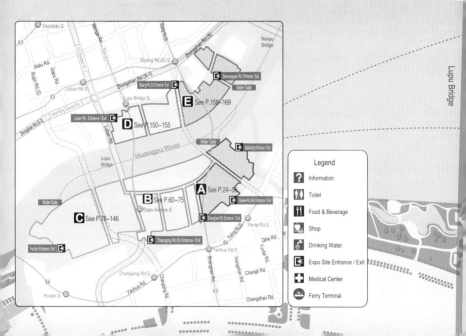

Legend

?	Information
🚻	Toilet
🍴	Food & Beverage
🛍	Shop
🚰	Drinking Water
➡	Expo Site Entrance / Exit
✚	Medical Center
⚓	Ferry Terminal

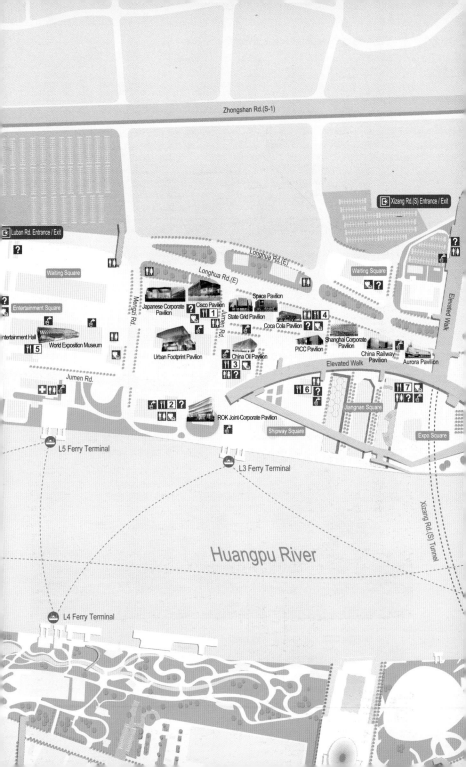

Zhongshan Rd.(S-1)

Xizang Rd.(S) Entrance / Exit

Luban Rd. Entrance / Exit

Longhua Rd.(E)

Longhua Rd.(E)

Waiting Square

Waiting Square

Entertainment Square

Space Pavilion

Japanese Corporate Pavilion

Cisco Pavilion **1**

State Grid Pavilion

Coca Cola Pavilion **4**

Entertainment Hall **5**

World Exposition Museum

Urban Footprint Pavilion

China Oil Pavilion **3**

PICC Pavilion

Shanghai Corporate Pavilion

China Railway Pavilion

Aurora Pavilion

Mengzi Rd.

Jumen Rd.

Jumen Rd.

Elevated Walk

Elevated Walk

6

7

Jiangnan Square

ROK Joint-Corporate Pavilion **2**

Shipway Square

Expo Square

L5 Ferry Terminal

L3 Ferry Terminal

Xizang Rd.(S) Tunnel

Huangpu River

L4 Ferry Terminal

Aurora Pavilion

Theme: **Chinese Jade Culture, New City Styles**

Day of Special Events: October 16

The pavilion takes the shape of L, the initial letter of the phonetic transcription of a Chinese character meaning "courtesy and integrity". Mainly colored ivory white, it looks like a large precious jade. The two 6-meter-high jade statues on the roof are modelled on the 2500-year-old Hongshan Jade Figure. Traditional jade making techniques will be presented to visitors.

- Visitors can have close contact with three robots named "Aurora Boys".
- In the theatre, a 3-D film on Goddess who patches the hole in the sky will be played.
- Exhibits include a 2.5-ton jade carving finished in the 1960s, as well as dozens of jade wares from Aurora Museum's collection.

Zone D

China Railway Pavilion

Theme: **Railway Brings Better Life**

Day of Special Events: October 2

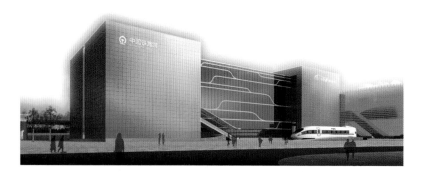

The exterior design of the pavilion uses metal and glass curtain walls to represent the City and uses panchromatic LED light to represent railway networks. Its three exhibition areas present China's latest innovations in the railway to emphasize the railway's role in urban development.

- The first exhibition area presents the milestones for China's railway.
- The second exhibition area shows visitors the railway construction in China.
- The third exhibition area uses models and devices to bring visitors an interactive experience.

China Oil Pavilion

Theme: **Oil, Extending City Dreams**

Day of Special Events: July 30

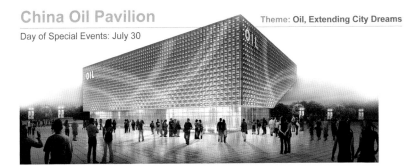

The pavilion's exterior is composed of interwoven oil pipelines like a huge energy processing network, indicating the role of oil as the major driving force of a better city. A new type of oil derivative is used as the building material. Divided into the front, major, and rear exhibition areas, the pavilion aims to present various ways of the evolution of oil, its role in urban development, both in the past and in the future.

- The 4000m^2 exterior wall will turn into a LED display varying with the sound of fountain music.
- Multimedia devices will create fantastic scenes of the oil and petrochemical industries.
- In a 4D cinema, visitors will be presented a 8-minute film about the evolution of oil.

D

Zone

Cisco Pavilion

Theme: **Smart + Connected Life**

The pavilion has a straight-line structure with its exterior colored green, blue, yellow and red. In the pavilion, an experience area for intelligently inter-connected solutions and Cisco's model "City of 2020" are designed to show the role of network services in optimizing resource utilization and to interpret its ideas on transport, energy, architecture, education, etc.

- A telepresence-based tour of "smart + connected life" will start with the warm welcome from virtual receptionists.
- A short film tells a story about how a family in Shanghai respond to a sudden storm, showing how technology may change people's life in the future.

Coca Cola Pavilion

Theme: **Coca-Cola and Expo 2010, A World Refreshed with Happiness**

Day of Special Events: May 8

The pavilion is a two-storey building whose exterior is metal shutters colored Coca-Cola red to prevent wind and rain. The pavilion is divided into five parts: Coca-Cola bottles showed outdoors, theatre, exhibition hall, VIP lounge and self-experience area, of which the aim is to present visitors a healthy and happy lifestyle and promote people's green awareness.

- Coca-Cola bottle show will give visitors unique sensation and various performances will also be staged.
- In the Coca-Cola theatre, a special video clip will be shown to help visitors better understand the theme of the pavilion.

Japanese Industry Pavilion

Theme: **Better Life from Japan**

The pavilion has a mesh structure of 10 000 pipes joined by 10 000 screw nuts. Its interior is decorated with recyclable pipes. All the images on the screen change every three minutes and visitors may move ahead in response to the change.

- A 18-meter-high and 10-meter-wide high-definition screen is used for the theme exhibition.
- The restaurant on the first floor will give the visitors high standard Japanese cuisine.
- In the shopping area, a post office of the future will trigger discussions on tomorrow's communication technology.

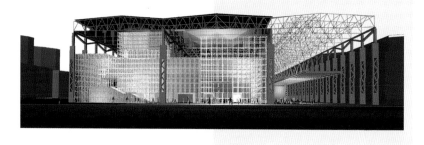

PICC Pavilion

Theme: **Beautiful Life: Stories of Love and Sharing**

Day of Special Events: October 20

The pavilion is a single-storey building with a sloping roof. Its main structure is the PICC logo and its exterior is colored bright white and red as well as Expo-logo green.

- The pavilion includes one axis, two wings and three areas, showcasing the functions and roles of the modern insurance industry.

- Interactive multimedia devices within the pavilion will show cartoons and promo videos.

D

Zone

Republic of Korea Business Pavilion

Theme: **Green City, Green Life**

Day of Special Events: May 27

Inspired by traditional Korean Hat Dance, the pavilion's exterior takes a spiral shape of ripples. At night, the spiral shines alternately in green, red, yellow, white, and black. In the pavilion, 4-D screens and interactive programs are designed to present visitors green technologies and energy recycling that are closely related to urban life.

- Artificial snow falls outside the pavilion three times a day: morning, noon, and evening for 20—30 minutes each time.
- In the "Smart Home" area, visitors can experience the intelligent elements of life,

e.g. remote control of home appliances and means of transport decided by navigation system.
- After the Expo, the pavilion's exterior will be made into environment-friendly shopping bags for Shanghai citizens.

Shanghai Corporate Pavilion

Theme: **My City, Our Dreams**

Day of Special Events: May 4

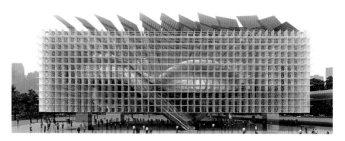

Named "Magic Cube", the pavilion is an intelligent and interactive eco-building. Visitors will have a 15-minute interactive tour in the pavilion featuring all-dimensional multimedia experiences and identifying with the theme of "My City, Our Dream."

- Industrial robots at the entrance will give performances and interact visitors via voice.

- In the 360° panorama theater, visitors will be led by Prof. Butterfly to a fantastic tour of interactions.
- Visitors will have the chance to enjoy over 1000 delicacies of the four Chinese cuisine styles which are prepared by robots.
- A lighting and music show will be presented before the pavilion closing every day.

D

Zone

Space Home Pavilion

Theme: **Harmonious Cities, People and Space**

Day of Special Events: October 15

The pavilion looks like a suspending magic cube in the immense universe supported by columns. Consisting of three sections of prelusive hall, theatre and scenarios, the exhibition centers around the idea of "heaven-earth-people" to show the role of aerospace technologies in creating a green, safe and intelligent home for mankind in the future.

- The prelusive hall "Origin of Dreams" will allow visitors to embark on a "space exploration".
- In the theatre "Spacewalk", visitors will be told a story about man and space.
- The "Beautiful Home" section consists of a space scenario embodying "Round Heaven" and a scenario of future intelligent city embodying "Square Earth".

State Grid Pavilion

Theme: **Innovation Empowers Dreams**

Day of Special Events: July 26

The central part of the pavilion is a crystal cube named "Magic Box", which shines day and night and can be seen in front of the pavilion, on the square or on the walkway afar. A 12-lense solar light device is used to provide lighting for the basement. The S-shaped passage is ingeniously designed to catch the summer wind in Shanghai.

- The Magic Box is a huge hexahedron which will immerse visitors in an audio and visual tour to experience the energy of nature and to explore the new life of future.
- Visitors can see through the transparent floor the "Heart of Energy", a high-tech transformer substation supporting the Expo Site and all the pavilions.

D

Zone

Location Diagram of Pavilions in Zone E

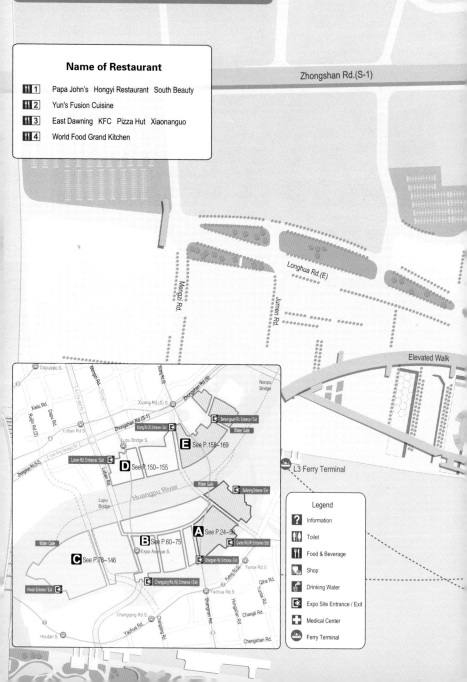

Name of Restaurant

🍴 1	Papa John's Hongyi Restaurant South Beauty
🍴 2	Yun's Fusion Cuisine
🍴 3	East Dawning KFC Pizza Hut Xiaonanguo
🍴 4	World Food Grand Kitchen

Zhongshan Rd.(S-1)

Longhua Rd.(E)

Mengzi Rd.

Jumen Rd.

Elevated Walk

L3 Ferry Terminal

Dapuqiao S.

Mengzi Rd.

Xizang Rd.(S)

Zhongshan Rd.(S)

Nanpu Bridge

Xietu Rd.

Rujin Rd.(S)

Dapu Rd.

Inner Ring Elevated Rd.

Xizang Rd.(S) S.

Zhongshan Rd.(S-1)

Xizang Xiu (S) Entrance / Exit

Bansongyuan Rd. Entrance / Exit

Water Gate

Zhongshan Rd.(S-2)

Luban Rd. S.

Lupu Bridge S.

Luban Rd. Entrance / Exit

E See P.158~169

Luban Rd.

D See P.150~155

Lupu Bridge

Huangpu River

Water Gate

Railway Entrance / Exit

A See P.24~56

B See P.60~75

Gaoxie Rd.(W) Entrance / Exit

Expo Avenue S.

Shangnan Rd. Entrance / Exit

Yantai Rd.S.

C See P.76~146

Pudong Rd.S.

Water Gate

Changqing Rd.(N) Entrance / Exit

Qihe Rd.

Houtan Entrance / Exit

Yaohua Rd.S.

Changli Rd.

Changqing Rd.

Shangnan Rd.

Hongshan Rd.

Yuotai Rd.

Changqing Rd.S.

Yaohua Rd.

Houtan S.

Chengshan Rd.

Legend

❓	Information
🚻	Toilet
🍴	Food & Beverage
🛍	Shop
💧	Drinking Water
➡	Expo Site Entrance / Exit
➕	Medical Center
⚓	Ferry Terminal

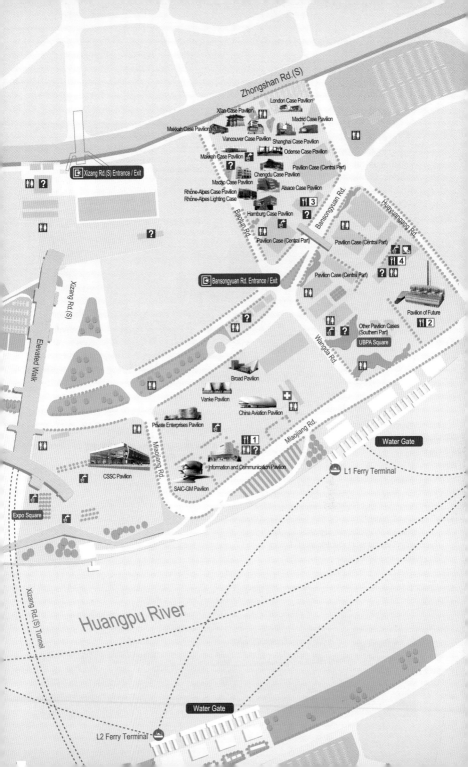

Zhongshan Rd.(S)

London Case Pavilion
Xi'an Case Pavilion
Madrid Case Pavilion
Makkah Case Pavilion
Vancouver Case Pavilion
Shanghai Case Pavilion
Odense Case Pavilion
Makkah Case Pavilion
Chengdu Case Pavilion
Pavilion Case (Central Part)
Macao Case Pavilion
Alsace Case Pavilion
Rhône-Alpes Case Pavilion
Rhône-Alpes Lighting Case
Hamburg Case Pavilion
3
Bansongyuan Rd.
Huayuangang Rd.
Baolian Rd.
Pavilion Case (Central Part)
Pavilion Case (Central Part)
4
Bansongyuan Rd. Entrance / Exit
Pavilion Case (Central Part)
Xizang Rd.(S) Entrance / Exit
Pavilion of Future
2
Other Pavilion Cases
(Southern Part)
UBPA Square

Xizang Rd.(S)

Wangda Rd.

Elevated Walk

Broad Pavilion
Vanke Pavilion
China Aviation Pavilion
Private Enterprises Pavilion
Miaojiang Rd.
Water Gate
1
L1 Ferry Terminal
CSSC Pavilion
Information and Communication Pavilion
Miaojiang Rd.
SAIC-GM Pavilion
Expo Square

Huangpu River

Xizang Rd.(S) Tunnel

Water Gate
L2 Ferry Terminal

Broad Pavilion

Theme: **Direction**

Day of Special Events: June 5

The pavilion, a white pyramid-shaped structure, consists of three parts of Demonstration Building, Triangle Hall and Outdoor Direct-fired Heater. Exhibitions focus on low-carbon and healthy lifestyle and the role of technology in environment protection. Artistic expressions, multimedia imaging and multidimensional representation are employed to create great visual impact of the pavilion as a whole.

- It takes just one day to finish the Demonstration Building, a unique exhibit for the Expo.

- In the Triangle Hall, a giant simulated globe, suspended in the air, is to showcase the scenes on global climate change. Nine image boxes of various styles are to display nine themes about environmental protection and relevant images.
- In the center of the outdoor square stands a direct-fired heater, part of which can display the ongoing operation in the machine. Visitors can watch closely how fire is used for cooling.

China Aviation Pavilion

Theme: **Aviation Connects Cities around the World**

Day of Special Events: September 21

Zone

The pavilion is built like a cloud, representing the dream of mankind to fly in the sky. It also looks like the mathematic symbol of infinity "∞", indicating the infinite development of aviation and the infinite changes that flying can bring to cities. The white membrane of the pavilion's exterior makes it easy for visitors to associate it with clouds and the ideas of flying.

- Visitors can experience the joy of piloting a plane in the flight simulator area.
- There is simulation of flying in clouds as well as a railcar running through the vast forest against lightning and thunder and then entering a beautiful city.

CSSC Pavilion

Theme: **Better Ship, Better City**

Day of Special Events: June 3

Converted from a former factory building, the pavilion has an arc structure resembling ship keel and dragon's backbone, symbolizing the indomitable spirit of Chinese national industry. The display of shipbuilding process and future ships will lead visitors to the future world of water so that they can experience in advance the life of future water city, and the close ties between human, shipping and cities.

- In the interaction area, visitors can make the ship they like by touching the screen according to the tips.
- A sightseeing corridor is built to set off the beautiful landscape in the Puxi Section.
- On the Shipbuilding History Avenue, model ships will be displayed to show China's long history of shipbuilding.

Information and Communication Pavilion

Theme: **Information and Communication — Extending City Dreams**
Day of Special Events: May 17

Focusing on "mobile information", the pavilion is in a streamlined shape without a corner in the entire building, symbolizing infinite communication. The exterior is illuminated with changing color patches and light bands to create a sparkling visual effect. The future of information and communication technology is presented to visitors in vivid stories shown on the huge theater screen.

- Visitors can use cell phones to take part in the activities in the dream garden in the waiting area.
- Visitors can talk to important figures in the history of communication through hand-held terminals, interacting with virtual figures.
- Visitors can use the solar photovoltaic charger in the pavilion to charge their cell phones at any time.

Zone

Private Enterprises Pavilion

Theme: **Vigour Matrix**

Day of Special Events: September 5

Composed of several large cylinders, the pavilion symbolizes the union of 16 Chinese private enterprises. The idea of "cell cluster" is used in the building to show the infinite power of cells growing from weak to strong. The inherent vitality of cells echoes the theme of the pavilion.

- "Intelligent film" used in the exterior can produce different visual effects as viewing and sunlight angles change.
- High technology is used to tell the true story about the growth of private enterprises, showing the multiplier effect created by the union of private enterprises.

SAIC-GM Pavilion

Theme: **Drive to 2030**

Day of Special Events: June 12

Inspired by car design, the pavilion takes a spiral shape, symbolizing the promising future of the auto industry. Visitors will be exposed to the vision of future urban mobility: zero carbon emission, zero traffic accident, little reliance on oil, little traffic jam, driving with fun, etc.

- The movie *Travel in 2030* tells a touching story about travelling in Shanghai in 2030.
- Visitors can write a letter to themselves or a friend and drop it into the Space Mailbox before its being received in 20 years.
- There is a 144° arc-screen, 488 zero-delay dynamic seats, new concept cars, etc.

Zone
E

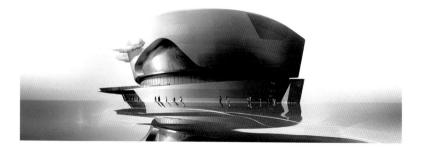

Vanke Pavilion

Theme: Possibility by Respect

Day of Special Events: September 20

The pavilion is composed of seven independent cylinder-shaped buildings made of wheat straw boards, around which there is 1000m^2 open water. Nicknamed "2049", it aims to present visitors what PRC's 100th birthday will be like. In the pavilion, five stories about termites, water, sand storm, waste and golden monkey are told to show the respect between human, nature and cities.

- Adventure to Termitary Hall shows visitors how human can learn from nature.
- Tree of Life Hall shows China's environmental protection campaign — forest restoration from farmlands.
- Mobius Strip Hall shows the daily actions of Taipei citizens in solving environmental problems.
- Elf of Snow Mountain Hall tells an adventure of golden monkeys saved from their lost living space.

Zone

Urban Best Practices Area (UBPA)

UBPA is to showcase recognized innovative practices of representative cities around the world in improving the quality of urban life and serves as a platform for cities to share experience in urban construction and development.

The Organizer of the Shanghai Expo set up an International Selection Committee to choose the practices from over 100 cases from across the world on livable cities, sustainable urbanization, conservation and utilization of cultural heritage and technological innovations in built environment which are worth exhibiting and promoting.

The UBPA is divided into the northern, central and southern parts. Built cases are exhibited in the simulated urban block in northern part on a scale of 1:1 so that visitors can experience better urban life in the future. Pavilion cases are exhibited in reconstructed workshops in the central part to share the experience in urban construction with visitors. Other cases are displayed in the southern case presentation halls in the forms of presentations, seminars, networks, display boards, events and performances.

E
Zone

Built Cases
(Northern Part)

Alsace Case Pavilion

Case Title: WaterSkin House

The prototype of the case is the solar wall of Bouxwiller High School in Alsace, a great example of using solar energy to keep interior temperature at a comfortable level. The water-skin solar wall on the southern elevation, controlled by computer, can open and close automatically as the outdoor temperature and sunlight intensity change, shading the sunlight and reducing energy use. There is a micro-brewery running on solar energy. Visitors can see the whole production process and have a taste of the newly-brewed beer.

Chengdu Case Pavilion

Case Title: Chengdu Living Water Park

The Chengdu Living Water Park is a water-themed urban ecological park. It can collect rainwater and sewage in communities and public space to be treated and recycled by the purification system, showing people how dirty and dead polluted water is turned clean and alive and inspiring people to cherish water resources. The case displays fully how the park is designed, how it works, and what it brings about.

Zone

Hamburg Case Pavilion

Case Title: Hamburg Sustainable New
            Building Project

The pavilion can keep room temperature around 25°C four seasons alike without air-conditioning and heating, and its energy use is only 10% that of an ordinary building. The 18-meter-high red-brick building, like a pile of drawers opening to four directions, takes a dual-role of a residential and office building. The 3D Wish Tree running through the entire building serves as a touring guide

to visitors, showcasing the future urban life Hamburg residents want and the government's response to the wish. Interactive programs will help to give visitors a full picture of Hamburg.

London Case Pavilion

Case Title: Zero-carbon Community

The prototype is BedZED the world's first zero-carbon community of Beddington where every house has an open garden or balcony, showcasing the perfect combination of high-density housing and comfortable life, and setting a new standard for energy-efficient buildings. The case pavilion reduces energy demand by installing energy-efficient facilities and achieves zero carbon emission by using renewable energy. Visitors will be exposed to zero-carbon auditorium, restaurant, showroom and six different styles of zero-carbon show houses as well as a series of activities of saving energy and cutting emissions.

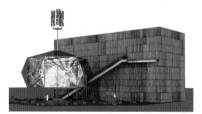

Macao Case Pavilion

Case Title: Restoration and Use of the Historical "Tak Seng On" Pawnshop in Macao

The prototype of the case is the century-old Tak Seng On Pawnshop which is now the first pawnshop museum co-built by the government and the private sector in Macao. The Expo Tak Seng On consists of Pawnshop Exhibition Hall, Important Figures Gallery and Macao Archive Hall. Multimedia is also used to tell the history of Tak Seng On and the story of its transformation into a pawnshop museum and cultural center. Jin Yong fans can find what they want from Jin Yong Collections.

Zone

Madrid Case Pavilion

Case Title: The Sample of Government Low-cost Housing Estate

The Madrid city council has been working on the largest public housing project in Europe over the last decade. Many green materials, advanced eco-technologies, and effective construction processes have been applied in the housing project. The most representative ones are the Bamboo House and Air Tree. The Bamboo House has various types of rooms to live which will make every visitor feel at home. Since the bamboo surface of different rooms opens in different ways at different time, the exterior of the entire building changes all the time. The Air Tree, right beside the Bamboo House, is a steel decagon structure whose roof is equipped with solar panels for energy supply.

Makkah Case Pavilion

Case Title: The Tents City of Mina: Best Urban Practice for Extreme Conditions

Massive inflow of pilgrims makes the Mina Valley of Saudi Arabia one of the world's most densely populated places. The case aims to show how to accommodate 3 million people in a 4km^2 area. The tent is made of a special material which is fire-proof, wind-proof, anti-corrosion, anti-skid and has a service life of 25 years. It only lets in 10% sunlight to ensure a comfortable temperature in the tent. Visitors will be presented with a model of the entire Tents City, the world's largest artificial reservoir as well as the projects to protect the city from mudslide and flood. Performances will be presented to visitors.

Ningbo Case Pavilion

Case Title: Tengtou Village—Urbanization and Ecological Harmany

The practice of Tengtou Village in Ningbo, Zhejiang is the only rural UBPA case of the Shanghai Expo. Tengtou is a successful example of urbanized villages in China. It seeks to strike a balance between developing tourism and protecting the eco-environment. The pavilion consists of several featured areas including Sounds of Nature, Close to Nature, Moving Images, Interactive Signature, etc. The concept of Sounds of Nature is inspired by the 24 solar terms of China. In the Close to Nature area, visitors can experience the environment and rich rural flavor of Tengtou.

Zone

Odense Case Pavilion

Case Title: The Revival of the Bicycle

The case is about the practice of Odense in promoting cycling. The exhibition area is like the "sun face" in the fairy tale of Hans Christian Anderson. State-of-the-art interactive technologies will be used to facilitate the participation of visitors. Various activities will be held in the central area like opening a children's cycling school. A demonstration cycling road will be built and traffic control facilities will be set up to simulate real situation. Odense may also provide some bicycles to be used in UBPA so that visitors will be able to tour the area by bike, which is environmentally friendly.

Rhône-Alpes Case Pavilion

Case Title: Bioenergy & Sustainable Housing in an Urban Environment

The case pavilion of Rhône-Alpes region of France is a four-storey building. Its building material is a type of recyclable baked clay. The design of staggered floors makes it easier to move between floors and survey all exhibition areas. The vegetation roof can purify air, adjust temperature, and drain rainwater in rainstorm. The rose garden in front of the pavilion shows visitors the most lovely classical and modern roses in France. There is a business center, restaurants and a famous French cooking school where visitors can watch chef cooking and have a taste of authentic French cuisine.

Rhône-Alpes Lighting Case Pavilion

Case Title: Lighting Cities of Region Rhône-Alpes

The case is about the experience of the Rhône-Alpes region in developing energy-efficient lighting system. Green lighting technology will be used to create fantastic night scene. Different lights will be put together to produce different patterns. Audio and visual effect will be enhanced with moving lights and sounds. One scheme is to produce a firefly-shaped lightings which fly down and light up the Expo Site. At the same time, a Light Show will be staged with the least energy consumption.

Zone

Shanghai Case Pavilion

Case Title: Eco-building Demonstration in Shanghai

The prototype of the case pavilion is a demonstration eco-building in Minhang District, Shanghai. As the first zero-energy building in China, it uses a huge solar thermal equipment to provide energy for the entire building. Green and energy-saving technologies to integrate solar energy in the building and make full use of rainwater and sewage, natural ventilation, shallow geothermal energy, display the concept of eco-housing and the pursuit of universal livable housing. The building has a shading system composed of shutters, French-window curtains and balcony awnings. Flowing liquids in the blue tubes on the wall can adjust the temperature of the entire building.

Vancouver Case Pavilion

Case Title: Legacies and the Livable City

Canada is among the world's most livable cities. False Creek in southwest Canada was where the Vancouver Expo was held in 1986 and is now one of the most dynamic and attractive districts in Vancouver. The southeast part of False Creek will be the Olympic Village for the Winter Olympics and Paralympics in 2010. The case of Winter Games will be presented at the Shanghai Expo to visitors to show Vancouver's experience in developing a livable city.

Xi'an Case Pavilion

Case Title: Daming Gong Relics Site: Protection and Surrounding Area Development Project

The Daming Gong (Daming Palace) is a political, economic and cultural center of the Tang Dynasty. In 1950s, China began the archaeological excavations of Daming Palace in the principle of protecting cultural heritage, improving surrounding environment and enhancing residents' living standard, setting a good example of achieving the harmonious coexistence of cultural heritage and urban life. Visitors will have a fantastic 3D experience of touring the palace as it was 1300 years ago. In interactive programs such as "Seek Treasures in Daming Palace", visitors can feel the cultural charm of the palace and China's ancient capital Xi'an.

Cases in Pavilion (Central Part)

Case	Case Title
Suzhou	Protection and Renovation of Suzhou Old City
Venice	Protection and Utilization of Historical Heritages: Urban Best Practices in Venice
Liverpool	Protection and Utilization of Historical Heritages in Liverpool
Cairo	An Integrated Model for Revitalization of Historical Cities
Hangzhou	The Water Control Practices of "Harnessing Five Waters" with West Lake at the Core to Construct "Quality Hangzhou"
Pondicherry	Achieving Economic and Environmental Goals through Heritage Preservation Initiatives as Demonstrated through: Asia Urbs Programme 2002-2004
Montreal	The Complexe Environnemental de Saint-Michel (CESM): A practicable example for the world

Case	Case Title
Bremen	From Knowledge to Innovation: Urban Transportation Solutions
Freiburg	Quartier Vauban — New Residential District for Freiburg
Guangzhou	Sustainable Urban Development — Water Environment Management
ENEA	Sustainable Italian-Style Cities
Rotterdam	Rotterdam Watercity
Sao Paulo	Clean City Project
Tianjin	Huaming Model Town — Tianjin, China
Dusseldorf	Business Meets Lifestyle — Livable City and Sustainable Development as Strategic Goals and Achievements
Porto Alegre	Governance Practice Based on Social Consensus: Strategies for Social Integration Promotion
Ahmedabad	Urban Governance Initiatives of Ahmedabad
Alexandria	Alexandria City Development Strategy
Seoul	Seoul Culturenomics
Bologna	Bologna: Creativity & Inclusion in the City
Shenzhen	Dafen Village — the Regeneration of An Urban Village in the City
Prague	Modern City Protecting Its Heritage
Malmo	Urban Sustainable Development Projects in a Former Industrial City
Geneva/ Zurich/ Basel	Better Water, Better Urban Life
Osaka	A City of Good Environment: The Challenge of the Water Metropolis, Osaka
Bilbao	Bilbao Guggenheim Museum: the Leading Project in Urban Strategy
Paris	A River, A Scenic Spot, A Lifestyle
Beijing	Olympic Village
Barcelona	I : The Old Town in the Center of Barcelona
	II : The District of Innovation
Hong Kong	Smart Card, Smart City, Smart Life
Izmir	The Aqueducts Reconstruction Project: Sewerage Disposal Project
Taipei	I : A City of Resource Recycling
	II : Wireless Broadband — A City of Convenience

Zone E

Other Cases (Southern Part)

Case	Case Title
île-de-France(Paris)	I : Sustainable Development of the City: Strategy and Governance
	II : Making the Historical City in the Future
	III : Restoring and Developing the Legacies of the Sustainable City
Brest	Sea World Exhibition
Bonn-Bukhara	Energy Conservation Starts from Children
Luxor	Karnak and Gurna Development Project
San Francisco	Global Warming: A Case for Sister City Cooperation in Finding Local Solutions for National Models
Victoria	Classroom of the Future
Wroclaw	The City of Leisure
Rosario	The Management and Construction of Public Space on the River Shore in the City of Rosario
Hannover	Expo 2000 Exhibit "Kronsberg District" — Ten Years After
Yanbian	Green Ecological "Golden Triangle" in North-East Asia — Harmonious Family of Multi-nationalities
Dongguan	Engine of Sustainable Development
Guangzhou	Green Land Action
Foshan	The Foshan Mode of Transmission of Civilization — Foshan Ceramic Culture in the Past, Present and Future
Zhongshan	Charities and Harmony — Better Urban Life
Wuzhen	Wuzhen — Legacies Protection
Kunshan	The Four Charms of Kunshan, Eco-Orientation Inspiring the City Vigor
Yangzhou	Protection of the Ancient City
Zhouzhuang	Water Story, Water Town
Xiamen	Cozy City and Garden on the Sea — Xiamen "Livable Community" Impression
Tangshan	An Ecological Rehabilitation Project in Southern Coal Mining-induced Subsidence Area of Tangshan
Rotterdam	Rotterdam, Watercity
Hong Kong	Smart Card, Smart City, Smart Life
Bremen	From Knowledge to Innovation: Urban Transportation Solutions
Odense	Spinning Wheels — The Revival of the Bicycle
Rhône-Alpes	I : Bioenergy & Sustainable Housing in an Urban Environment
	II : Lighting Cities of Region Rhône-Alpes
Liverpool	Protection and Utilization of Historical Heritages in Liverpool
Barcelona	The District of Innovation

Zone

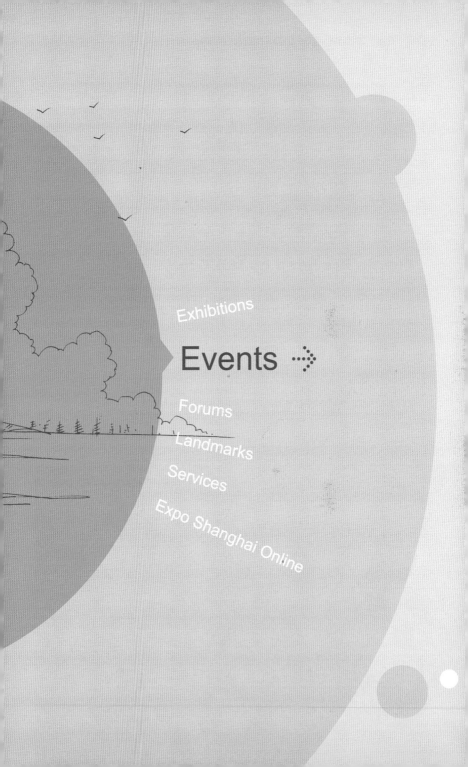

Exhibitions

Events ⟶

Forums

Landmarks

Services

Expo Shanghai Online

Exciting and innovative events play a significant role in making the Expo "successful, splendid and unforgettable".

During the Shanghai Expo, lots of performances will be staged. Events to be held in Pudong and Puxi are defined as "Global Classic" and "Future Creativity" respectively.

These events will be held either at indoor venues in the Expo Site, including Expo Center, Bao Steel Stage, Expo Culture Center and Entertainment Hall, or outdoors at Squares of Asia, Africa, Europe, Americas and Oceania, Exposition Square, Houtan Square, UBPA Square and two large docks.

The spectacular float parades, a dazzling array of performances, primitive jungle dances and gala shows will add the festive atmosphere to the Expo Site.

Events Provided by the Organizer

The Organizer will stage four categories of events: ceremonies, parades, stage performances and theme performances. Ceremonies include the Opening Ceremony, Opening of the Expo Site, National Day of China Pavilion, closing activities and the Closing Ceremony.

Parades, stage performances and theme performances include:

Pageants

Description: Pageants — a series of spectacular parades that echo the theme of the Shanghai Expo, will be held several times a day during the Expo.
Time: May 1 — October 31,2010
Venue: Expo Site

Theme Show: *Window of the City*

Description: In line with the Expo theme, it shows the evolution of urban life through fantastic settings and stunt performance and tells a story about "love, harmony and touching moments".

Time: 3-4 shows every day, each lasting 30 minutes

Venue: Houtan Square (Zone C)

Performance by China Oriental Song and Dance Ensemble

Description: The performance is a large music and dance show specially designed for the Shanghai Expo, and consists of *Colorful World, Splendid China* (both temporarily titled), etc.

Time: 2 shows every day, Monday — Friday

Venue: Expo Culture Center (Zone B)

Acrobatic drama: *Cha Show*

Description: The acrobatic drama specially designed for the Shanghai Expo will make its debut during the Expo. Martial arts, magic, stunts, songs and dances are combined to interpret the particular charm of Chinese tea culture.

Time: 4 shows every day, each lasting 45 minutes, May 1 — June 30, 2010

Venue: Entertainment Hall (Zone D)

Shaolin Kung Fu Play: *Legend of Shaolin Monks*

Description: Produced for the Shanghai Expo, the play is a stunning show of *Shaolin Kung Fu*, dances and acrobatics.

Time: 4 shows every day, July 1 — August 31, 2010

Venue: Entertainment Hall (Zone D)

Wudang Kung Fu Play: *Wudang — Tai Chi Tao*

Description: Produced for the Shanghai Expo, the play provides an interesting interpretation of Chinese Taoist culture, including its rituals, Wudang Kung Fu and Taoist regimen.

Time: 3 shows a day, July 1 — September 30, 2010

Venue: Slipway Square (Zone D)

China Elements

Description: This event is a mix of performances, exhibitions, learning and interactive sessions. It shows excellent performing arts, traditional skills and handicrafts in China.

Time: May 1 — October 31, 2010

Venue: Bao Steel Stage (Zone B)

Expo Chorus Festival

Description: 2010 performers from outstanding international choirs, student choirs of music conservatories and local choirs in Shanghai will sing famous choruses and songs in the evening of July 21.
Time: July 21, 2010
Venue: Expo Culture Center (Zone B)

UBPA Square Festival

Description: 22 street performance teams from across the world will offer cheerful and interactive performances in waiting areas for some of the most popular pavilions and Group Level Squares. This will achieve the double purposes of entertaining the audience and controlling visitor flows.
Time: 20 shows a day, each lasting 20 minutes
Venue: 7 Group Level Squares, waiting areas outside popular pavilions, and public areas

Abilia

Description: It is designed for teenagers to experience 20 representative future jobs via entertainment and interaction.
Time: 6 experience sessions a day, each lasting 90 minutes
Venue: Dock 3, Jiangnan Square (Zone D)

Rod-puppet show: *Journey to the West*

Description: Based on the classic Chinese novel *Journey to the West*, the puppet show tells, from an interestingly new perspective, the story of Monkey King.
Time: May 1 — June 30, 2010
Venue: Dock 1 (Zone D)

Shadow play: *Romance of the Three Kingdoms*

Description: Based on the classic Chinese novel *Romance of the Three Kingdoms*, the shadow play tells, from an interestingly new perspective, the story of Zhuge Liang.
Time: July 1 – August 31, 2010
Venue: Dock 1 (Zone D)

Children's Multimedia Show: *Magic Map of Sesame Street*

Description: Haibao and the animated characters in the famous TV show *Sesame Street* as the heroes, this show is both educational and entertaining.
Time: 2 shows a day, each lasting 30 minutes
Venue: Dock 1 (Zone D)

Multimedia Show: *Haibao Is Coming*

Description: It combines multimedia technology and the performance of real actors. The hero Haibao will take visitors on a fascinating tour of future cities.
Time: 2 shows a day, each lasting 30 minutes
Venue: Dock 1 (Zone D)

Interactive experience program: *We Are the Family*

Description: Specially made for the Shanghai Expo, this program tells the story of how three families in Shanghai, Milan and Tokyo overcome geographic barriers to enhance family bonds and communication.
Time: May 1 — October 31, 2010
Venue: Houtan Square (Zone C)

Innovative Tours of Youth

Description: It includes a series of interactive activities based on 100 innovative projects, which the Organizer recruited in such fields as new energies, materials, technologies, thinking and services.
Time: May 1 — October 31, 2010
Venue: Houtan Square (Zone C)

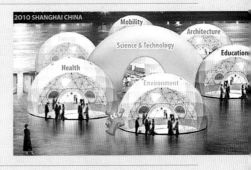

Youth Series Events

Description: Consisting of theme shows and cultural exchanges, these youth-oriented events are innovative, interactive and entertaining. They try to highlight the youth's pursuit for better cultural life in cities and the use of the square as a cultural venue.
Time: 3 shows a day, each lasting 60—90 minutes
Venue: Exposition Square (Zones D & E)

Events by Participants

Events held by participants mainly include National Day events, Honor Day events, events for Theme Week of Province/Autonomous Region/Municipality, and special events. Some of them are listed below.

National Day events

Each participating country may choose one day during the Shanghai Expo to hold events in the Expo Site.

Continent	Country	Event	Venue
Asia	Japan	"Traditional and modern" festival performance	Expo Center, Expo Culture Center (Zone B)
	Lebanon	*Two Thousand and One Nights* by Caracalla Dance Group	
	Israel	David D'or Concert	
Europe	United Kingdom	Performance by Royal Ballet	
	France	France Music Festival	
	Finland	Musical: *Spin*	
Americas	Venezuela	Performance by Simon Bolivar Symphony Orchestra	
	Canada	Performance by Circus of the Sun	
	Brazil	MAWACA body percussion	
Africa	Burundi	Burundi drum show	
	Cape Verde	Concert of "Barefoot Diva" Cesaria Evora	
	Cameroon	Performance by Cameroon National Song and Dance Troupe	
Oceania	Samoa	National group dance	
	Solomon Islands	Pan flute performance	
	Fiji	Traditional songs and dances	

Honor Day events

Each participating international organization may choose one day during the Shanghai Expo to hold events in the Expo Site.

International organization	Event	Venue
United Nations	"Night of Innovation"	Expo Center, Expo Culture Center (Zone B)
International Committee of the Red Cross	"Red Cross" Global Charity Star Concert	
World Meteorological Organization	Performances by weathermen from across the world	

Events for Theme Week of Province/Autonomous Region/Municipality

Each Chinese province/autonomous region/municipality may hold five-day events in specified venues in the Expo Site based on the Organizer's schedule.

Province	Event	Venue
Hebei	Wuqiao acrobatics, Hebei martial arts stunt and folk dances	Bao Steel Stage, Celebration Square, western section of Bocheng Road (Zone B)
Shanxi	Drum music	
Inner Mongolia	Mongolian wedding; performances by Hulun Buir Fantasy	
Shaanxi	Dance *Prosperous Tang Dynasty*; drum dance *Folk Custom*	
Tibet	Tibetan dramas and songs	
Shandong	Taishan Worship Ceremony or Qufu Confucius Worship Ceremony; group drum music	

Special events

Each participating city in UBPA may hold special events under the requirements on Honor Day events.

City	Event	Venue
Bremen	Bremen Chamber Symphony Concert; acrobatic ballet	Expo Center (Zone B), UBPA Square (Zone E), Exposition Square (Zones D, E), Entertainment Hall (Zone D)
Liverpool	Royal Liverpool Philharmonic Orchestra Concert	
Osaka	Folk dances celebrating Sino-Japan friendship	
Taipei	Symphony Orchestra Concert	
Rhône-Alpes	Performances by Lyon street artist group	

(Note: for all the events, please refer to the announcement on the day of performance.)

Exhibitions

Events

Forums ⇢

Landmarks

Services

Expo Shanghai Online

As one of the three major parts of the Shanghai Expo, forums are closely related to its thematic concept and messages. They deal directly with its theme, and serve as an important platform to demonstrate the legacy of previous world expositions and to envision future ones.

In addition to exhibitions which demonstrate human civilization and innovative ideas, forums are held during the Shanghai Expo to discuss on hot urban issues and find possible solutions.

With public forums held one year before its opening, the Shanghai Expo will see one summit forum and six theme forums.

Summit Forum

The summit forum is planned to be held on October 31, 2010 in Shanghai.

Themed on "Urban Innovation and Sustainable Development", it will allow attendees to discuss on global challenges associated with sustainable urban development.

About 1500 people, including Chinese government leaders, UN Secretary General and Deputy Secretary General, BIE President and Secretary General, heads and ministers of foreign states, some mayors at home and abroad, representatives of relative international organizations, Commissary-General of Exhibition areas, and representatives from business, academic and other circles will attend the forum.

Shanghai Declaration, an important document based on a consensus on global urban development issues reached by the participants of the Shanghai Expo, will be issued.

Theme Forums

Elite professionals from home and abroad will gather together to communicate on issues related to sustainable urban development and offer strategic proposals for the development of cities of all types.

The theme forums will be held in Nanjing, Suzhou and Wuxi of Jiangsu Province and Hangzhou, Ningbo and Shaoxing of Zhejiang Province.

Theme forum I: Information Technology and Urban Development

Time: May 15-16, 2010
Location: Ningbo, Zhejiang Province

The rapid development of IT leads people into an era of information and makes informatization a natural choice for cities. The forum focuses on urban management, life and integration and envisions the future of cities in the context of informatization.

Theme forum II: Cultural Heritage and Urban Regeneration

Time: June 12-13, 2010
Location: Suzhou, Jiangsu Province

Cultural issues related to urban construction and development will be discussed from six perspectives, namely inheritance of tangible culture and preservation of intangible culture, integration of diverse urban cultures and cross-cultural communication, creative culture and cultural ecology, thus offering references for the cities of developing countries.

Theme forum III: Science & Technology Innovation and Urban Future

Time: June 20-21, 2010
Location: Wuxi, Jiangsu Province

Urban development and technological innovation always supplement each other. This forum will deliver its own explanation on the roles of technological innovation in safeguarding city security, driving sustainable development, enhancing urban competitiveness and creating better life.

Theme forum IV: Urban Responsibilities during Environmental Changes

Time: July 3-4, 2010
Location: Nanjing, Jiangsu Province

Cities, as the breeding grounds for various environmental problems, suffer the consequences most directly. Environmental protection, climate change, energy efficiency and emission reduction require the concerted efforts of government, enterprises and citizens.

The forum centers on six topics: cooperation between cities in addressing environmental changes, comprehensive improvement in urban environment, green industries and innovation in production pattern, enterprises' environmental and social responsibilities, publicity and popularization of green concepts, sustainable life and consumption modes.

Theme forum V: Economic Transformation and Urban-rural Relations

Time: September 9-10, 2010
Location: Shaoxing, Zhejiang Province

Economic transformation is an issue confronted by most countries. Developed countries need to upgrade their industrial structures, while developing countries are under the pressure of industrial and economic restructuring, particularly the transformation from traditional agricultural society to a modern industrial one. China has the world's largest rural population, and both its successes and failures in balancing urban-rural development may provide other developing countries with helpful ideas. This topic is of even relevant today given the global financial and food crises.

Theme forum VI: Harmonious City and Liveable Life

Time: October 6-7, 2010
Location: Hangzhou, Zhejiang Province

In the era of urbanization, a sustainable urban environment has become increasingly important for liveable life. This forum aims to explore more effective methods for cities to better meet people's requirements and the effective mechanism for sound urban development and liveable life, so as to promote the well-being of humanity.

Centering on urban space, society and environment, discussions will be held on regional coordination, supporting systems, urban community, housing policies, built environment and social security to explore the relationship between harmonious city and liveable life.

Public Forum

Public forums consist of Youth Forums (including Youth Summit Forum), Provincial Forums, Shanghai District Forums, Culture and Media Forums, Women & Children Forums, etc. Except for Youth Summit Forum, etc. most forums were held before the opening of the Expo.

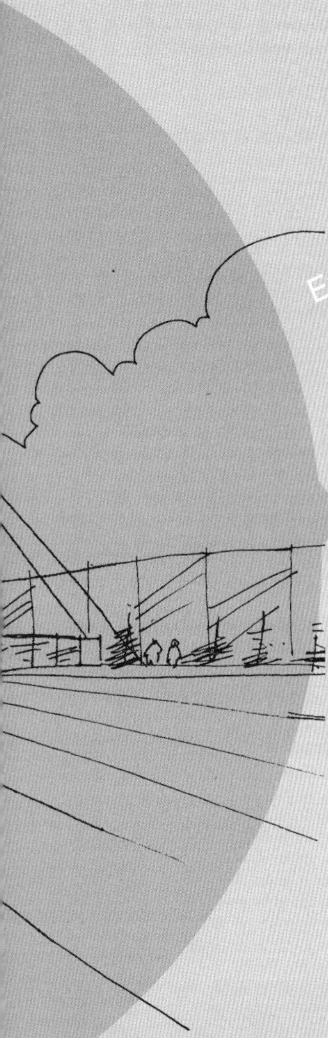

Exhibitions

Events

Forums

Landmarks ⋯▸

Services

Expo Shanghai Online

In addition to amazing pavilions, the Expo Site also boasts a number of landmarks including Expo Center, Expo Culture Center, Expo Axis and other important buildings for such purposes as conferences, performances, transportation, leisure, catering and services. These signature buildings interpret, in their own ways, the theme of "Better City, Better Life".

Expo Center

The Expo Center, on the north of the Expo Avenue and west of the Expo Axis in Zone B, will host the summit forum, ceremonies, VIP receptions and press releases during the Shanghai Expo.

The exterior design of the building is simple yet elegant. With an impressive glass-curtain facade, it resembles a huge crystal palace. As a venue for conferences, receptions and other events, the building is well equipped to meet varying requirements.

Divided into Green Hall (central hall), Red Hall (auditorium for 2600 people), Blue Hall (international conference hall for 600 people), Golden Hall (banquet hall for 3000 people) and Silvery Hall (7200m^2 multi-functional hall as the main press center), the Expo Center is a wonderful example of panorama buildings.

The Blue Hall features a 14m-high power-operated door which many heads of state and other international celebrities will go through during the Expo. Thus the door is named as "the door of the world".

As an outstanding example of green building, the Expo Center adopts many energy conservation technologies such as solar energy, LED lighting and rain collection.

These green and low-carbon concepts and technologies, an important part of Expo legacy, will surely contribute to future urban construction initiatives.

Expo Axis

Expo Axis (1000m×110m) in Zone B extends from the main entrance of the Expo Site to the Celebration Square and is the biggest structure in the Site.

With two stories above ground and another two underground, it is the main route within the Expo Site. It is connected with the four permanent pavilions and offers catering, entertainment, commercial and conference services.

The Expo Axis is decorated with six inverted-cone shaped steel structures, the Sun Valleys. They allow in sunlight and fresh air, easing the feeling of oppression that may be easily aroused in an underground space and at the same time saving energy.

Beside the Sun Valleys, another attractive feature of the Expo Axis is the white "umbrellas" on its top, which make up the world's biggest stretched membrance supported by fixed cables.

Expo Culture Center

The Expo Culture Center, located in Zone B, resembles a UFO in shape. It may take on various forms from different angles and at different times. It is like a lovely sea shell in daytime and a floating city at night.

Having two floors underground and six floors above ground, it is used for most performances during the Expo.

In addition to large celebrations and concerts, large-scale international sporting events,such as NBA basketball matches and international hockey games, also can be held here.

The seat capacity of its main venue can be adjusted between 18 000, 12 000, 8 000 and 5 000 based on performance demand.

World Exposition Museum

The World Exposition Museum in Zone D will allow visitors to trace the 150-year history of the world exposition and great steps forward in human civilization.

In the front lobby, small-size replicas of 15 signature buildings of previous expositions such as the Crystal Palace and the Eiffel Tower will be exhibited. Made entirely of "gems", they sparkle brilliantly under the lights.

Also on display are 12 Expo mascots, including Haibao, who are able to sing and dance.

The exhibition on history of world exposition includes precious exhibits at the first world exposition (provided by Victoria and Albert Museum), and Ferris Wheel that debuted in the US. The sketch drawing for Picasso's "Guernica" will also be on show.

Expo-related songs will be played in the "Expo Music Box", offering visitors a superb audio-video experience.

BIE (Bureau of International Exhibitions) Tree shows the history of BIE and bidding procedures for world exposition.

Bao Steel Stage

Located in Zone B, the Bao Steel Stage is one of the indoor performance venues for the Shanghai Expo. Events for Theme Week of Province/ Autonomous Region/ Municipality and other ceremonies will be staged.

The original facilities of Bao Steel factory have been modified as the large stage, highlighting the concept of enviroment-friendliness.

Thanks to its proximity to Lupu Bridge and its semi-open structure, the stage offers a wonderful view of the Huangpu river and the Expo Site. Indeed, it is a stage that can "breathe".

Entertainment Hall

The Entertainment Hall in Zone D features a glass-curtain facade and a semicircle interior structure. The innovatively-designed red spectatory is encased in the glass lounge, like a diamond glittering in a crystal box. The roof lighting system evokes a dreamlike atmosphere at night.

Acrobatic drama *Cha Show* will be staged here from May 1 to June 30, 2010.

Visitors will enjoy martial arts, magic, songs and dances full of Chinese flavor.

The *Shaolin Kung Fu* play specially designed for the Shanghai Expo will be performed here, four times a day from July 1 to August 31. The play tells the growth story of a young monk, and introduces the spectators to the Shaolin Kung Fu and Buddhist meditation.

Bailianjing Garden

Bailianjing Garden lies in the north of the Expo Site in Pudong and adjacent to the Expo Park in the west.

The garden is designed in the concept of "rippling", which symbolizes, among others, the gradually-gained serenity after impact and the integration after breakdown.

The 1560m-long coastline of the garden and the reconstructed 13 docks on the opposite bank form a unique waterfront landscape.

Houtan Garden

Houtan Garden is the sole wetland garden in the Expo Site.

The garden is dotted with various plants that blossom in different months, such as peach, pear and pomegranate, etc. Besides, crops that are rarely seen in cities are planted here to present attractive rural scenery.

Over 20 types of aquatic plants form a natural filter system that could purify 2400m^3 river water a day without the help of any chemicals or specialized equipment.

Expo Garden

The Expo Garden is the main riverside green space in the Expo Site.

Drawing inspiration from "bund" and designed based on the environment-friendly concept, the Expo Garden rises from the bank of the Huangpu River and extends like a Chinese folding fan.

Arbor trees on the upper level of the garden and roads, bushes, facilities and venues on the lower level are perfectly combined to make up a lovely landscape.

The six precious Eastern firs are highlights of the garden.

Given the city's hot summer, the garden uses wind corridors, spraying, vertical greening and other technologies to create a refreshingly cool environment for visitors.

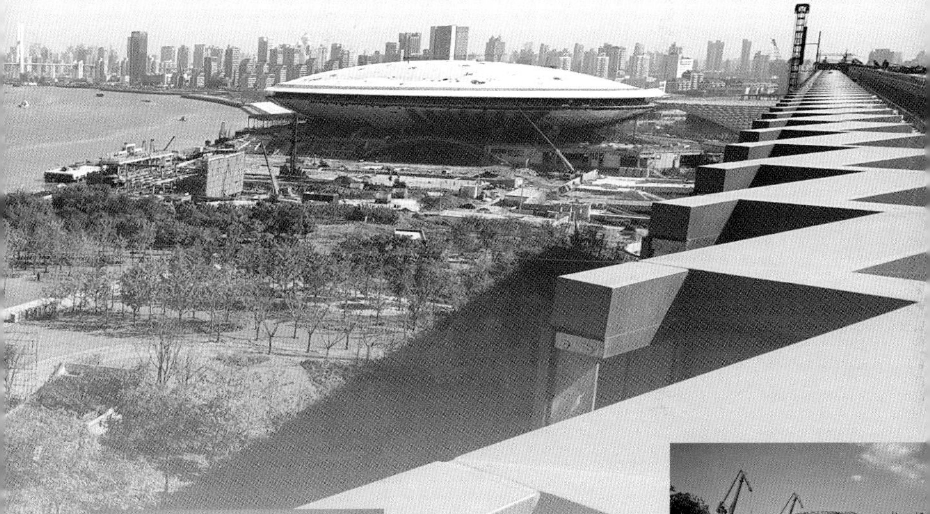

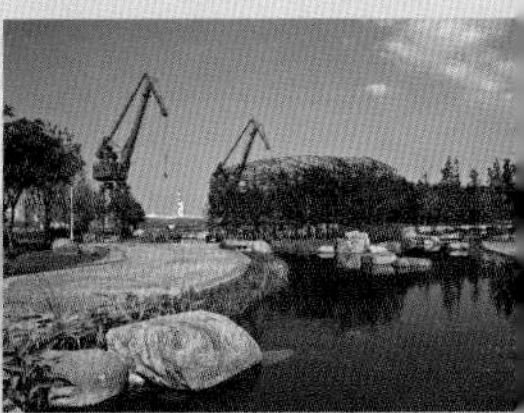

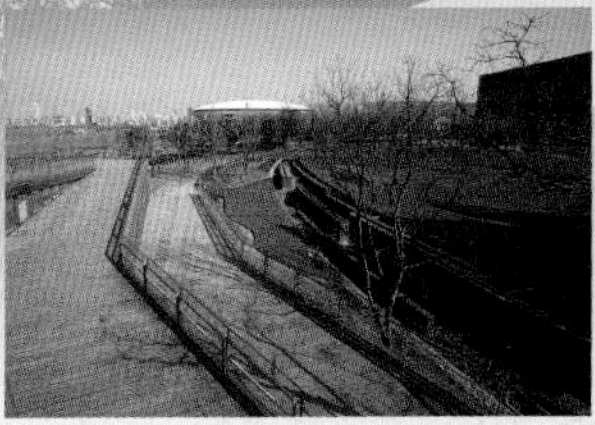

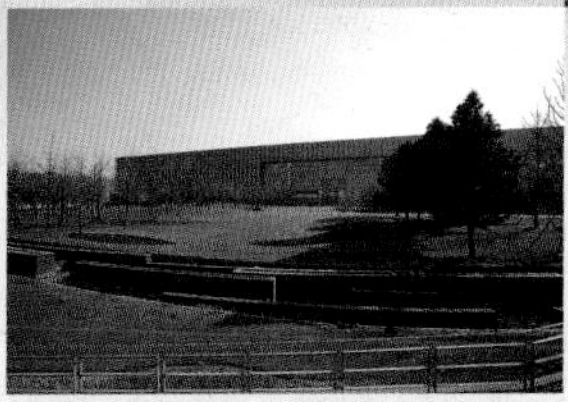

Exhibitions

Events

Forums

Landmarks

Services

Expo Shanghai Online

Ticketing

Ticket purchase

Tickets will be sold through Expo outlets, designated agents and Expo Site tour operators etc.

Domestic visitors may purchase tickets from China Mobile, China Telecom, Bank of Communications and China Post via their outlets, websites, telephones or customer managers.

Overseas visitors may buy tickets from designated Expo ticket agents on their own countries or regions.

The Expo Bureau designates some Expo Site tour operators in domestic provinces for group tours. People interested may call their offices or log in to their websites.

From May 1, 2010, people can purchase tickets (except for peak day admission) via on-site ticket offices and automated ticket machines, etc.

The Expo Bureau may post ticket information on the official website www.expo2010.cn. For the latest information, the public may access the website or dial +86-21-962010.

Phase / Type	Pre-sale Phase I 2009.3.27— 2009.6.30	Pre-sale Phase II 2009.7.1— 2009.12.31	Pre-sale Phase III 2010.1.1— 2010.4.30	Expo-time 2010.5.01— 2010.10.31
Peak Day·Single Day Admission	¥170	¥180	¥190	¥200
Peak Day·Special Admission	N/A	N/A	¥110	¥120
Standard Day·Single Day Admission	¥130	¥140	¥150	¥160
Standard Day·Special Admission	N/A	N/A	¥90	¥100
3-Day Admission	N/A	N/A	¥400	¥400
7-Day Admission	N/A	N/A	¥900	¥900
Evening Admission	N/A	N/A	N/A	¥90
Group Admission	Only available for designated Expo Site tour operators			
Student Group Admission	Only available for designated Expo Site tour operators and educational institutions			

Ticket types

The nine types of Expo tickets are either individual or group tickets shown as follows:

Category	Type	Policy	Notes
Individual Ticket	Peak Day Single Day Admission	For all visitors; on the designated day or any standard day; one ticket per person, valid for one entry only.	Peak days include Labor Day Holiday (May 1-3, 2010), National Day Holiday (October 1—7, 2010), and one week before the closing date (October 25 — 31, 2010), 17 days in total.
	Peak Day Special Admission	For the disabled, people born in or before 1950, full-time students on regular higher education programs, high school programs and compulsory education programs, children above 1.2m, and all Chinese military personnel on active service. Valid IDs are required upon ticket purchase and entry; on the designated day or any standard day; one ticket per person, valid for one entry only.	
	Standard Day Single Day Admission	For all visitors; on any standard day other than peak day; one ticket per person, valid for one entry on the day of admission to the park.	
	Standard Day Special Admission	For the disabled, people born in or before 1950, full-time students on regular higher education programs, high school programs and compulsory education programs, children above 1.2m and all Chinese military personnel on active service; valid IDs are required upon ticket purchase and entry; on any standard day other than peak day; one ticket per person, valid for one entry on the day of admission to the park.	For all visiting days (167 days in total) except for peak days during the Expo.
	3-Day Admission	For all visitors; valid for any three days except peak days; one ticket per person, valid for one entry per day.	
	7-Day Admission	For all visitors; valid for any seven days except peak days; one ticket per person, valid for one entry per day.	
	Evening Admission	For all visitors; entry after 17:00 except peak days; one ticket per person, valid for one entry on the day of admission to the park.	
Group Ticket	Group Admission	For groups with no less than 15 people; tickets should be purchased in advance and reservation is required before entry; valid for one entry on the day of admission to the park.	Not directly available for the public. Group admission tickets are sold via designated Expo Site tour operators as a kind of Expo tourist product, and those for students in the form of student tourist products or via educational institutions.
	Student Group Admission	For groups with no less than 30 students on regular higher education programs, high school programs and compulsory education programs; except peak days; tickets should be purchased in advance and reservation is required before entry; valid for one entry on the day of admission to the park.	

Except for children at or under 1.2m, a ticket is always required for a visitor to the Expo Site.

Unless otherwise specified, people with the Expo tickets can visit all the pavilions within the Expo Site.

Ticket Samples of Shanghai Expo

Standard Day • Special Admission

Standard Day • Single Day Admission

Peak Day • Single Day Admission   Peak Day • Special Admission

3-Day Admission   7-Day Admission

Transportation

To the Expo Site

For visitors' convenience to the Expo Site, Shanghai is constructing a comprehensive urban transport system and an Expo public transport network which enables visitors to reach the Expo Site via rail transit, bus and water transportation.

There is 1 metro line entrance/exit, 8 ground entrances/exits, 4 extra-Site and 3 intra-Site water gates.

Metro Line Entrance/exit	
Puxi Section	Madang Road Station of Metro Line 13
Ground Entrance/exit	
Puxi Section	Entrance/exit at Luban Road, South Xizang Road, Bansongyuan Road
Pudong Section	Entrance/exit at Bailianjing, West Gaoke Road, Shangnan Road, Changqing Road, Houtan
Water Entrance/exit	
Extra-Site Water Gate	Dongchang Road Water Gate, Qichangzhan Water Gate, Shiliupu Water Gate, Qinhuangdao Road Water Gate
Intra-Site Water Gate	Dock 1 (Miaojiang Road • Wangda Road) Dock 2 (Expo Avenue • Bailianjing Road) Dock 6 (Houtan Garden)

Intra-Site Transport

On most occasions, visitors can get to pavilions on foot in the Expo Site.

Since the Expo Site is divided by the Huangpu River and there is quite a distance between the zones, the Organizer sets up a public transport system including metro line, bus and cross-river ferry.

Metro Line	Metro Line 13 is designed to facilitate visitors' travelling between Pudong and Puxi Sections. There are Madang Road Station, Lupu Bridge Station, and Expo Avenue Station on the line.
Ground Transport	Five bus routes, including two sightseeing routes, are designed to facilitate visitors' touring in Pudong or Puxi Section and travelling between the two sections.
Water Transport	Five ferry routes are designed to facilitate visitors' travelling between Pudong and Puxi Sections.

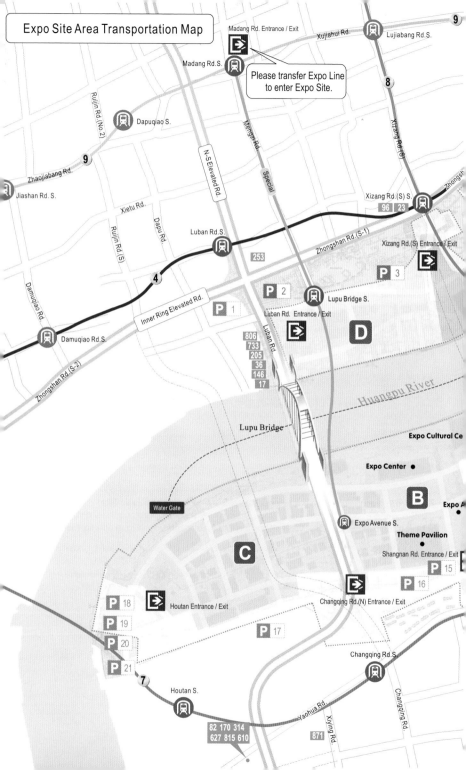

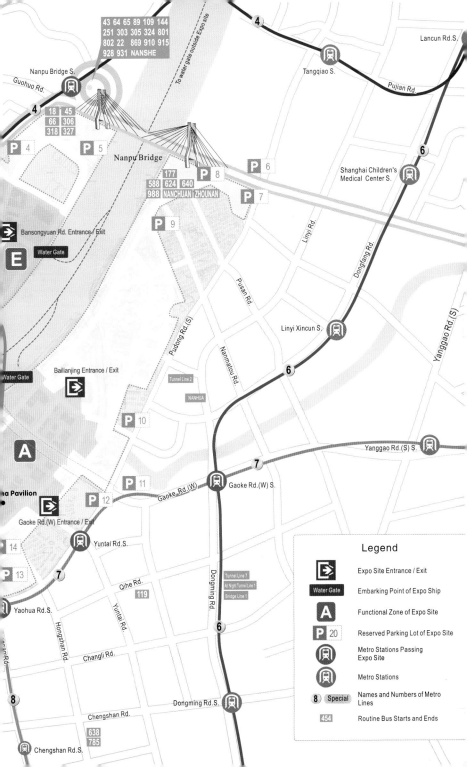

43 64 65 89 109 144
251 303 305 324 801
802 22 869 910 915
928 931 NANSHE

4

Lancun Rd.S.

Tangqiao S.

Pujian Rd.

Nanpu Bridge S.

Guohuo Rd.

4

18 | 45
66 | 306
318 | 327

P 4   P 5

Nanpu Bridge

P 8

P 6

6

Shanghai Children's
Medical Center S.

177
588 | 624 | 640
988 NANCHUAN ZHOUNAN

P 7

P 9

Linyi Rd.

Dongfang Rd.

Bansongyuan Rd. Entrance / Exit

E Water Gate

Pusan Rd.

Linyi Xincun S.

Water Gate

Bailianjing Entrance / Exit

Pudong Rd. (S)

Nanmalu Rd.

Tunnel Line 2

NANHUA

6

Yanggao Rd.(S)

Yanggao Rd.(S) S.

P 10

A

7

P 11

Gaoke Rd.(W)

Gaoke Rd.(W) S.

P 12

na Pavilion

Gaoke Rd.(W) Entrance / Exit

Yuntai Rd.S.

14

Dongming Rd.

Tunnel Line 7
All Night Tunnel Line 1
Bridge Line 1

P 13

Qihe Rd.

Yuntai Rd.

119

Yaohua Rd.S.

Hongshan Rd.

Changli Rd.

6

8

Dongming Rd.S.

Chengshan Rd.

638
785

Chengshan Rd.S.

Legend

	Expo Site Entrance / Exit	
Water Gate	Embarking Point of Expo Ship	
A	Functional Zone of Expo Site	
P 20	Reserved Parking Lot of Expo Site	
	Metro Stations Passing Expo Site	
	Metro Stations	
8 Special	Names and Numbers of Metro Lines	
454	Routine Bus Starts and Ends	

To water gate outside Expo site

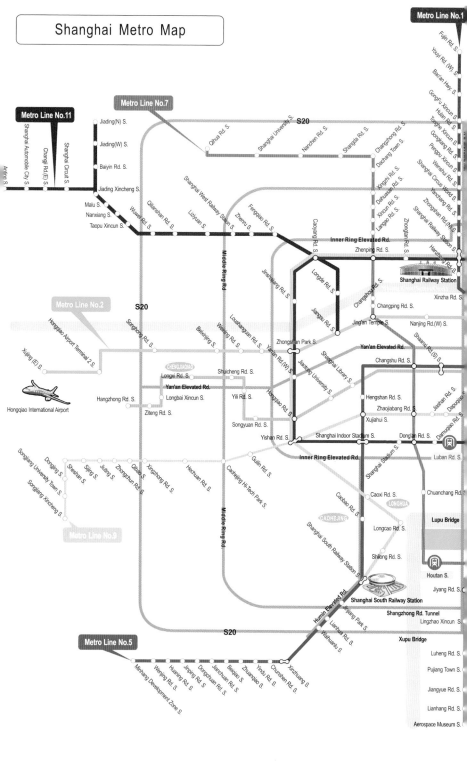

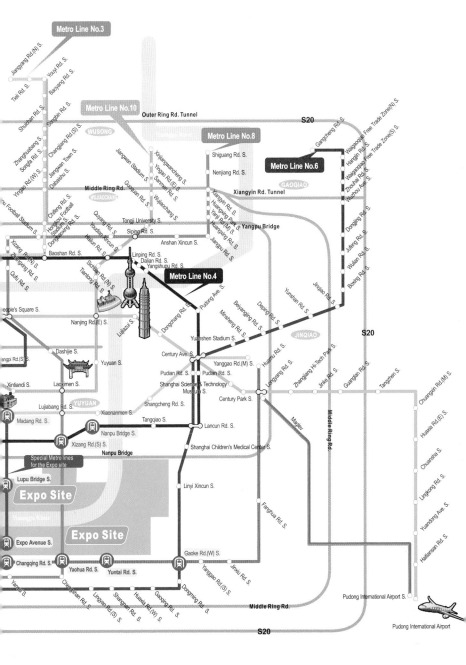

Metro stations passing Expo Site   O Metro transfer stations
Data updated as of March 10th, 2010, is subject to actual operation

Catering

The Shanghai Expo is also a food fair for all the visitors. Delicacies from across China and the world are available at catering service points in the Expo Site, and restaurants are set in some national pavilions to serve specialties and snacks.

Many restaurants are opened in the five zones and the Expo Boulevard, offering Chinese, Western and Japanese cuisines and fast food.

The Catering Center, to the west of the Expo Boulevard, divided into different zones serving cuisines of various countries, is the biggest catering establishment in the Expo Site.

Zone A

Major restaurants

Name of restaurant	Type of catering service	Estimated cost per person (RMB)
KFC	Western fast food	25-45
Be For Time Tea House	Chinese casual dining	30-35
Blue and White Restaurant	Chinese fast food	30-35
Bianca	Japanese fast food	30-50
Bamboo	Chinese fast food	30-50
Yoshinoya	Japanese fast food	35
Ajisen Ramen	Japanese fast food	35-50
Yuesheng Restaurant	Chinese fast food	35-50
Zabon	Japanese fast food	35-80
Hongchangxing	Muslim cuisine	40
Pakistan Restaurant	Muslim cuisine	40-60
Ogawaya	Japanese fast food	50-60
Godly	Vegetarian meal	60

Zone B

Major restaurants

Name of restaurant	Type of catering service	Estimated cost per person (RMB)
Fresh-pure Chinese Fast-food	Chinese fast food	20-30
Chinese Food Plaza	Food court	20-40
Cheerway	Chinese fast food	30
Kozuka	International cuisine	30-50
Shanghai Local Flavors Area	Chinese fast food	35-40
Zabon	International cuisine	35-80
Colabo	Italian casual dining	40-100
Latino Restaurant	International cuisine	50
CP Food Pavilion	Western casual dining	50-100
Anjile	International cuisine	50-150
Heji Xiaocai Restaurant	Chinese cuisine	80-100
Food Plaza of Xinghualou Group	Chinese cuisine	100
Relax Turkish Restaurant	International cuisine	100-150
Laozhengxing Restaurant	Chinese cuisine	100-150
Deyuelou	Chinese cuisine	100-150
Zhiweiguan Restaurant	Chinese cuisine	100-150
Tongqinglou Restaurant	Chinese cuisine	100-150
Majesty Plaza Shanghai	Chinese cuisine	100-150
Courtyard by Marriot Shanghai Pudong	Chinese cuisine	100-150
Huatian Restaurant	Chinese cuisine	100-150
Chao Food Restaurant	Chinese cuisine	100-150
Sichuan Folk	Chinese cuisine	100-150
Le Provencal-Merry Hotel	International cuisine	150
Xiaonanguo	Chinese cuisine	150
Yicai Restaurant	Chinese cuisine	150-500

Zone C

Major Restaurants

Name of restaurant	Type of catering service	Estimated cost per person (RMB)
Uncle Fast Food	Chinese fast food	20
Zkungfu	Chinese fast food	20-25
Daniang Dumpling	Chinese fast food	20-30
KFC	Western fast food	25-45
East Dawning	Chinese fast food	25-45
Canglangting	Chinese casual dining	30
Yuyuan Restaurant	Food court	30-40
Cel	Japanese fast food	30-40
Food Plaza of Xinghualou Group	Chinese cuisine	30-40
Haquna Matata African culture restaurant and pub	African cuisine	30-200
Burger King	Western fast food	36
Manabe	Cafe	40
Jade Cuisine	Chinese fast food	40
Newcom Tea Theme Restaurant	Chinese casual dining	40-50
Pizza Hut	Western casual dining	40-150
MX Hong Kong	Food court	45
Starbucks Coffee	Cafe	45
Tenya	Japanese fast food	45
Duck King	Chinese cuisine	48
Wishdoing	Chinese fast food	50
Pleasant Turkish Restaurant	Western fast food	50-60
Irish Stout	beerhouse	50-100
Bulgarian Restaurant	Western casual dining	50-100
Uruguay Restaurant	Western casual dining	50-100
Jade Garden	Chinese cuisine	50-250
Papa John's	Western fast food	55-80
Airest	Western casual dining	70
Harvest Festival Zhejiang Restaurant	Chinese cuisine	70
C-straits Steak/Coffee Restaurant	Cafe	70
Hai Ku Japanese Restaurant	Japanese fast food	80-100
Red Chicken	Chinese cuisine	80-100
South Beauty	Chinese cuisine	200-260

Zone D

Major
Restaurants

Name of restaurant	Type of catering service	Estimated cost per person (RMB)
Dinglianfang	Chinese casual dining	10-50
Ming Hong-Tangyang Congou Black Tea	Tea	10-150
Shendacheng Restaurant	Chinese fast food	15
Wufangzhai	Chinese fast food	15
Yinuo Coffee	Cafe	15-50
Lihua Fast Food	Chinese fast food	20-30
Hanamaru	Japanese fast food	20-40
Jiji Town	Chinese fast food	25-30
Wafumura	Japanese fast food	25-30
KFC	Western fast food	25-45
Laofengge Pinzhenxuan	Chinese cuisine	25-150
Yungho Soybean Restaurant	Chinese fast food	30-35
Zkungfu	Chinese fast food	30-35
Hongchangxing	Muslim	40
Pizza Hut	Western casual dining	40-150
Osaka · Sakai's Pu	Japanese fast food	50-100
Hesheng Tea Banquet	Tea	58-400
Wumi Porridge	Chinese cuisine	60
South Beauty	Chinese cuisine	80-120
Asahibeer Restaurant	Beerhouse	80-150
Zagara	Western casual dining	98-328
Jade Garden	Chinese cuisine	120
Bao Steel Hotel Restaurant	Chinese fast food	140-200

Zone E

Major
restaurants

Name of restaurant	Type of catering service	Estimated cost per person (RMB)
World Food Grand Kitchen	Food court	10-35
KFC	Western fast food	25-45
East Dawning	Chinese fast food	25-45
Hongyi Restaurant	Western fast food	30-50
Pizza Hut	Western casual dining	40-150
Papa John's	Western fast food	60-80
Yun's Fusion Cuisine	Chinese cuisine	70
South Beauty	Chinese cuisine	80-120
Xiaonanguo	Chinese cuisine	150

Expo Axis

Major
restaurants

Name of restaurant	Type of catering service	Estimated cost per person (RMB)
RBT Food & Beverage (Shanghai) Limited	Chinese casual dining	15
85°C Café	Bakery	20-25
Croissants de France	Bakery	25
KFC	Western fast food	25-45
East Dawning	Chinese fast food	25-45
Christine	Bakery	25-50
Manabe	Cafe	30-40
Caiyunjian	Tea	30-45
Burger King	Western fast food	35
Mister Donut	Cafe	35-50
Dicos	Western fast food	40
Mu Creative Bakery	Bakery	40-50
Master Kong Chef's Table	Chinese fast food	45
Starbucks Coffee	Cafe	45-50
Dain Ti Hill	Chinese casual dining	50-100
Xinyi Restaurant	Western fast food	50-70
Papa John's	Western fast food	55-80
Chamate	Chinese casual dining	65
Afternoon Tea	Cafe	70-80
TOT.Taste of Taiwan	Chinese cuisine	70-100
Wangbaohe Pudong	Chinese cuisine	100-200
South Beauty	Chinese cuisine	200-260
German Big Steak	Western cuisine	100-200

Shopping

The franchised products of the Shanghai Expo include garments, stationery, gifts, toys, shoes and hats, bags and suitcases, gold and silver commemorative coins, etc. Visitors can buy unique Expo souvenirs and gifts in retail stores in public areas within the Expo Site. Besides, foreign countries also set up shops within their pavilions to sell souvenirs of national or pavilion features.

Visitor services

To make the touring in the Expo Site pleasant, the Organizer offers various services for the visitors, including information and reception, visit guidance, visit reservation, signage, rental, infant and child service, assistance for the disabled, lost and found, and first-aid etc.

Information and Reception	Information desks are set within the Expo Site and at entrances/exits to offer information and consultancy.

- Offer information on schedules and venues of exhibitions and events in the Expo Site
- Provide consultancy on weather, transport and restaurants in the Expo Site
- Release manuals and maps
- Accept visitors' suggestions, complaints and claims

Visit Guidance	Guidance stations are set at main passages in the Expo Site such as entrance/exit squares, elevated pedestrians' walk, the Expo Boulevard and main roads to offer guidance and consultancy, control visitor flow and maintain the order.

- Offer visit consultancy
- Control visitor flow
- Hand out documents, assist the disabled, report medical emergency and give directions to a destination.

Visit Reservation	Offer group reservation and on-site individual reservation for pavilions and events.

- Group visitors may reserve online via the group ticket purchaser
- Individual visitors may make reservations for pavilions or events at reservation terminals when entering the Expo Site, and those who have a reservation made can enter the pavilions or event venues at specified time.

Signage	An effective sign system can tell visitors the overall layout of the Expo Site, give directions to a destination, and provide other information including pavilion operation.
Rental	Visitors may rent wheelchairs, audio guides, navigation devices, pushchairs, etc. in main service point in the Expo Site and return them to the same point.
Infant and Child Service	Look after lost children; receive loss report and carry out searches; provide tidy waiting and breast-feeding rooms for visitors with babies. ● Accept lost children under 14, handle visitors' request for searching lost children, release information on lost children and carry out searches. ● Offer waiting and breast-feeding rooms for visitors with babies.
Assistance for the Disabled	Build a barrier-free Expo Site with helpful staff and specialized facilities, offering convenient and considerate services for the disabled. ● Equipment rental for the disabled ● Information desk handling the report on the loss of the disabled.
General Public Service	Offer postal, financial, meteorological and other services. ● Postal service: souvenirs, commemorative stamps, mail and express, etc. ● Financial service: currency exchange, ATM and counter facilities, etc. ● Meteorological service: real-time temperature, warning about thunderstorm, typhoon and high temperature, three-day weather forecast, etc.
Lost and Found	Offer registration and release of lost and found information as well as claiming of lost property.
First Aid	First aid stations offering free services are set up in the Expo Site by the Shanghai Municipal Bureau of Public Health and the Chinese Red Cross Society. Patients in serious medical conditions will be transferred promptly to designated hospitals outside the Expo Site.

Volunteers

EXPO 2010 **Volunteer**

The ingeniously designed volunteer logo resembles the Chinese character "心" (meaning "heart"), the letter V (for volunteer) and a dove with an olive branch in its beak. In showcasing the unique Chinese culture, it also reflects the warm-heartedness of volunteers. The iridescent colors and flying ribbons symbolize cordial hospitality of Shanghai. The slogan of the volunteers is At Your Service at EXPO.

By category, there are Expo Site volunteers and information booth volunteers. The services of the former mainly include information, visitor flow management, reception, translation and interpretation, visit assistance, and assistance in media service, event and forum organization. The latter are stationed in 2000 information booths across Shanghai to offer services including information, translation, interpretation and first aid.

Volunteer Dress

世界在你眼前，我们在你身边
At Your Service at EXPO

城市有我更可爱
Our City, Your Joy

2010，心在一起
2010, We're Together as One

志在，愿在，我在
My Will, My Help, My Pleasure

Exhibitions

Events

Forums

Landmarks

Services

Expo Shanghai
Online ⇢

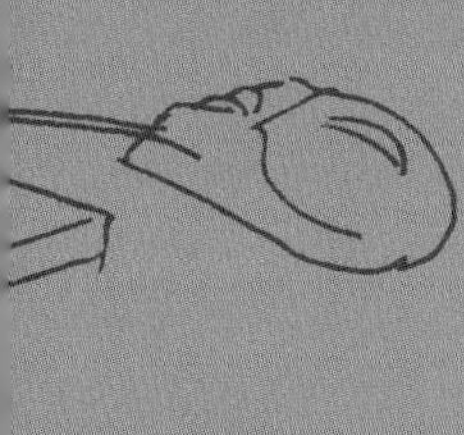

Expo Shanghai Online

www.expo.cn

As an important part of the Shanghai Expo, Expo Shanghai Online has been available in Chinese and English. It provides a three-dimensional and panoramic view of the Expo Site and pavilions, allowing netizens to tour the Expo Site and enter virtual pavilions to appreciate all exhibits and exhibition items.

"Site Tour", as the core of the Expo Shanghai Online, shows over 100 pavilions in the five zones and their exhibits and exhibition items three-dimensionally. Here, people can view a pavilion's exterior from different angles, tour around the pavilions and closely appreciate exhibits. And as an added bonus, some online pavilions would display a number of exhibits that cannot be found in physical pavilions.

"City of Future" is a 3D interaction and entertainment platform showing the most distinctive pavilions in the Expo Site. Netizens may embark on a virtual tour of the Expo Site and learn about the history of world exposition through interesting stories and games. Besides, they have a chance to visit together with image ambassadors of the Shanghai Expo and to win Expo souvenirs and tickets. They may also participate in building future cities with their own imagination.

In Expo Ferris Wheel, there are interesting stories about the Expo, and interpretations on the Expo theme, as well as online Expo movies. In Expo Carnival, netizens can play the game of Expo Wizard or leave their own messages; Community is where visitors can share their views on the Expo.

图书在版编目（CIP）数据

中国2010年上海世博会官方导览手册：英文版／ 上海世博会事务协调局编.
——上海：东方出版中心，2010.4
ISBN 978-7-5473-0154-8
Ⅰ.中⋯ Ⅱ.上⋯ Ⅲ.博览会—上海市—2010—手册—英文
Ⅳ.G245-62

中国版本图书馆CIP数据核字（2010）第046906号

CIP Data

Expo 2010 Shanghai China Official Guidebook/ Compiled by Bureau
of Shanghai World Expo Coordination
——Shanghai: Oriental Publishing Center, 2010.4
ISBN 978-7-5473-0154-8
Ⅰ.Chinese... Ⅱ.Shanghai... Ⅲ.Expo—Shanghai City—2010
—Guidebook—English Ⅳ. G245-62

National Library of China CIP Data No. 046906-2010

Edited by Expo 2010 Shanghai Magazine
Produced by Project Team from China Publishing Group Corporation
Mapped by Shanghai Surveying and Mapping Institute

Expo 2010 Shanghai China Official Guidebook
Compiled by Bureau of Shanghai World Expo Coordination

China Publishing Group Corporation
Oriental Publishing Center
(345, Xianxia Road, Shanghai 200336 www.orientpc.com)
China Translation and Publishing Corporation
(A4 Chegongzhuang Street, Xicheng District, Beijing 100044
    www.ctpc.com.cn)
Issued by: Oriental Publishing Center
Printed by: Shanghai Donnelley Printing Co., Ltd.
Format: 787mm×1092mm   1/32
Printed Sheet: 7.5
Edition: First Edition in Apr. 2010 First Printed in Apr. 2010
ISBN 978-7-5473-0154-8
Price:RMB 25.00